**John Heil** is Professor of Philosophy at Washington University in St Louis, Professor of Philosophy at Durham University, and an Honorary Research Associate at Monash University. Professor Heil is a Fellow of the Australian Academy of Humanities and is listed among the 50 Most Influential Living Philosophers.

# What is Metaphysics?

# What is Metaphysics?

## John Heil

polity

First published in 2021 by Polity Press

Polity Press
65 Bridge Street
Cambridge CB2 1UR, UK

Polity Press
101 Station Landing
Suite 300
Medford, MA 02155, USA

ISBN-13: 978-1-5095-4648-0
ISBN-13: 978-1-5095-4649-7(pb)

A catalogue record for this book is available from the British Library.

Library of Congress Cataloging-in-Publication Data

Names: Heil, John, author.
Title: What is metaphysics? / John Heil.
Description: Cambridge ; Medford, MA : Polity, 2021. | Series: What is philosophy? | Includes bibliographical references and index. | Summary: "Metaphysics can be understood as the branch of philosophy that examines the fundamental nature of reality. In this textbook for students new to the topic, John Heil covers the key concepts in an original, jargon-free way" -- Provided by publisher.
Identifiers: LCCN 2021000205 (print) | LCCN 2021000206 (ebook) | ISBN 9781509546480 (hardback) | ISBN 9781509546497 (paperback) | ISBN 9781509546503 (epub)
Subjects: LCSH: Metaphysics.
Classification: LCC BD131 .H45 2021  (print) | LCC BD131  (ebook) | DDC 110--dc23
LC record available at https://lccn.loc.gov/2021000205
LC ebook record available at https://lccn.loc.gov/2021000206

Typeset in 11 on 13 pt Sabon by
Servis Filmsetting Ltd, Stockport, Cheshire
Printed and bound in Great Britain by CPI Group (UK) Ltd, Croydon

For further information on Polity, visit our website: politybooks.com

In memory of
David Armstrong, Charlie Martin, and Jack Smart

# Contents

# Preface

Metaphysics is, by my lights, a difficult, but indispensable, subject. Each of us harbors unexamined metaphysical preconceptions that might, or might not, survive serious scrutiny. This book aims to tease out those preconceptions in a manner that challenges you the reader to confront them. Many of your preconceptions are widely shared, and many, no doubt, are warranted even though you might not be in a position to vouch for them were you called upon to do so.

Socrates observed that an unexamined life was not worth living. He did not mean that a life worth living requires having all the answers. He meant that we should recognize what we know and what we only think we know: we should understand our limitations and what these might portend. This is the spirit in which I offer this book. The goal is not to parade a string of metaphysical doctrines past you and declaim their pros and cons. The goal, rather, is to encourage you to reflect on matters that, for most of us, most of the time, remain beneath reflection.

This is not a frivolous undertaking. Preconceptions spawn attitudes that color thoughts and actions, sometimes in surprising ways. Distinctively metaphysical attitudes are intertwined with attitudes we evince as we go about our business – in everyday life, in the arts, and in the sciences. The trick is to recognize them for what they are and thereby be in a position to take into account their influence – for good or ill – on the attitudes that govern our serious thoughts about the cosmos and our place in it.

This book approaches metaphysics, not as an academic subject to be mastered then forgotten, but as a hands-on exercise, the lasting value of which lies in the doing. For this reason, I have not tried to hide my own views, an impossibility in any event. That might be worrisome were it not the case that the views are the vehicles, not the destinations. If I succeed in persuading you that metaphysics, far from being a purely academic pastime, is unavoidable, I will be content. If I leave you better equipped to recognize hidden metaphysical themes for what they are, I will be delighted.

Although the book presupposes no prior acquaintance with metaphysics, I have tried to steer the conversation in ways that might engage even hardened academic philosophers. If you are among their ranks, you are hereby forewarned not to expect exhaustive treatments of individual metaphysical doctrines. There is a time and a place for everything, and this is neither the time, nor the place, for exhaustive treatments of anything.

John Heil
Melbourne
July 2020

# Acknowledgments

*What is Metaphysics?* took shape in Melbourne during my tenure as a Fulbright Fellow in the first half of 2020. I am much indebted to the Australian–American Fulbright Commission and to Monash University, my host institution, for their support. The Fellowship, which was meant to run from mid-February through June, was cut short by the onset of the Covid-19 pandemic, but I remained in Australia with my wife, Harrison, and continued working from our adopted home in Caulfield South thanks to the graciousness of Marie-Thérèse Jensen. My stay at Monash would not have been possible without the support of Christina Twomey, Head of the School of Philosophical, Historical, and International Studies; Jakob Hohwy, Head, Department of Philosophy; and Jessica Weijers, School Manager, who deserves a gold parking pass.

I would not be the philosopher I am, and this book would not have been the book it is, had I not enjoyed the company of ten philosophers who are no longer around to read these words: David Armstrong, Donald Davidson, Fred Dretske, J. J. Gibson (whom I count as a philosopher), Jonathan Lowe, Charlie Martin,

Norman Malcolm, Hugh Mellor, Mark Overvold, and Jack Smart.

Keith Campbell and John Bigelow, both important figures in Australian philosophy, have continued to exert a powerful gravitational pull on my thoughts, although not always in the same direction. I have also been influenced at close range by Jonathan Bennett, Alex Carruth, Randolph Clarke, Heather Dyke, Anthony Fisher, Frank Jackson, Jaegwon Kim, Anna Marmodoro, Yitzhak Melamed, Elizabeth Miller, Gonzalo Rodriguez-Pereyra, Peter Simons, Roy Sorensen, Galen Strawson, and Peter van Inwagen. I am most grateful to four anonymous readers who provided insightful advice and managed to convince me to temper my worst instincts, and to Ian Tuttle for finding and correcting numerous gaffes and infelicities. Harrison Hagan Heil suffered through successive versions of the book, offered invaluable counsel, and, more than anyone else, helped shape its character.

Pascal Porcheron, my editor at Polity Press, encouraged me to persevere in the project that resulted in this book. An old adage has it that the best way to learn something is to teach it. To the extent that this is true, it is true because you do not fully understand something until you can explain it to yourself, a prerequisite for teaching it to others. Writing this book afforded me the rare opportunity to do both, and for that I am especially grateful to Pascal and to Polity Press.

# 1

# Introduction

## 1.0 Metaphysics Is . . . What?

This book is addressed to readers curious about metaphysics. Today, purveyors of serious metaphysics reside in university philosophy departments, or, at any rate, would have spent time in academic settings. The book's aim, however, is to convince you that, far from being an effete academic pastime, metaphysics is inevitable. Each of us embraces metaphysical theses, often without recognizing them as such. Philosophers are not the only philosophers. What distinguishes card-carrying, capital-P Philosophers from everyone else is just that the Philosophers embrace metaphysical doctrines self-consciously.

Readers whose impressions of metaphysics stem from acquaintance with books featured on popular bookstore shelves bearing the label might have a somewhat different view of the subject. For those readers, metaphysics is likely to exude an aura of mysticism or maybe thoughts of tarot cards and astrological readings, coupled with a measure of unconstrained speculation. If, in picking up this book, this is what you were expecting, you might be alarmed – or relieved – to learn that the metaphysics to be discussed here comports with both hard-edged science and everyday experience. The Australians call this *ontologically serious* metaphysics.

So conceived, metaphysics has a long history, and a much longer prehistory. This is not a historical survey, however, but a foray into a subject matter that runs the historical gamut. One underlying theme is that, whether anyone likes it or not, metaphysics is pervasive. Self-proclaimed skeptics who dismiss metaphysics as a frivolous waste of time most often do so on the basis of unexamined metaphysical commitments of their own, commitments unlikely to survive honest scrutiny.

I will try to convince you of metaphysics' inevitability, not by argument, but, starting with this chapter, by example. Because the book is meant to draw in nonspecialists, its focus will be on broad theses and suggestive arguments, rather than on the fine-grained details of these theses and arguments. This is not a matter of dumbing down the subject. The Devil is in the details, but the chief interest in, and significance of, metaphysics lies less in the details than in the extent to which metaphysics provides satisfying proposals for solutions to issues that lie just below the surface of everyday life, the arts, and the sciences.

## 1.1 Metametaphysics

You might think that the place to begin would be with a definition of "metaphysics," a succinct characterization that would give you some idea of what you are in for. Would that it were so. Definitions of subjects – mathematics, psychology, poetry, for instance – rarely assist those looking for help in discerning the nature of the subject matter. To the extent that they are intelligible to the nonspecialist, definitions tend to be vague and impressionistic. Psychology is the study of human behavior. Yes, but how does this distinguish psychology from biology, anthropology, or marketing? When precise definitions are available, they are most often of interest only to those already familiar with the subject.

I could tell you that metaphysics is the study of being or the nature of reality, but that does not set metaphysics off from hosts of other subjects including, but not limited to, the sciences. I could tell you that metaphysics provides our most general characterization of what there is, leaving more specific characterizations to the various sciences. But again, this does little to distinguish metaphysics from physics, the most general of the sciences.

Some suppose that metaphysics is distinguished from the sciences in being a priori: metaphysics endeavors to derive truths about reality from truths that require no further warrant, truths that are self-evident. If you want a model, think of Euclidean geometry in which theorems are deduced from a small number of axioms purporting to be self-evident. Physics, in contrast, like the other sciences, relies on a posteriori reasoning that begins and ends with empirical observation and investigation.

As the example of Euclidean geometry suggests, however, characterizing metaphysics as relying exclusively on reason would fail to distinguish metaphysics from mathematics. Mathematics is essential to the sciences, but unlike metaphysics, it has no worldly pretenses. Its utility depends not on its capturing truths about reality, but in description and calculation. In its simplest form, calculation takes, as inputs, truths or purported truths, and yields outputs that must be true if the inputs are true.

In putting it this way, I am skating over scores of important features of mathematics. My aim is not to show how or why mathematics works, however, but only to note that, if metaphysics were a priori it would be in good company.

But *is* metaphysics a priori? Not by my lights. Although

metaphysics does not compete with the sciences – or, for that matter, with poetry or fiction – metaphysics seeks to provide a systematic account of categories indispensable to any endeavor to say what there is, and that is not something that could be arrived at by reason alone.

The last sentence is hopelessly abstract, but you can get a feel for what I have in mind by considering three historically central categories: substance, property, relation. Substances are objects possessing various properties and standing in various relations to one another. Take this tomato, a candidate substance. The tomato is a something that has various qualities, its properties. The tomato is red, roughly spherical, and has a definite mass, and stands in a variety of relations – the tomato is next to a beetroot, and on top of your kitchen counter.

## 1.2 Ontology

In embracing the categories of substance, property, and relation you would be betting that these would prove indispensable in any attempt to say *what there is*. Suppose you describe what is on the desk in front of you: a book, a pencil, and a tablet. (Your mobile phone is across the room.) To a first approximation, books, pencils, and tablets are propertied substances standing in assorted relations to one another. As you move further afield you encounter trees and rabbits, living substances. In front of you is a street sign, and a dustbin, and in the west the sun is setting. All of these things would seem to qualify as substances, all possess various properties and stand in various relations to one another, and to endless other things.

Moving beyond the everyday, you can find substances, properties, and relations in play in the sciences. Physics and chemistry speak of particles and atoms, for instance. Atoms themselves are made up of electrons, protons, and neutrons. These might be thought to be substances, possessing various properties (mass, charge, spin), and standing in assorted relations – spatial, temporal, causal.

Although we commonly take for granted that material bodies are made up of particles, we could be mistaken. What we treat as particles might turn out not to be granular, self-contained, mobile bits of matter, but to be energy concentrations in fields, or local thickenings in space. In that case, the fields or space itself would be the substances, and particles would turn out to be properties, modifications of fields or of space.

I mention these seemingly far-fetched possibilities only by way of example, only to illustrate the relation between the sciences, and particularly physics, and *meta*physics. At the heart of metaphysics is *ontology*. Ontology offers a systematic account of categories of being or reality. If an ontology of substances, properties, and relations were adequate, you could see these as serving as what C. B. Martin calls placeholders, the details being supplied by the various sciences. If material bodies are made up of particles, for instance, the particles would be the substances. If particles were replaced by fields, the substances would be the fields. The sciences have a way of surprising us, evolving unpredictably. Still, it is not easy to envision a scientific revolution that dispensed with propertied substances of some sort, however strange.

I have emphasized the relation of metaphysics to the sciences, but the sciences are not our only avenues to knowledge. Poetry, music, fiction, drama, and their cousins have much to teach us. What distinguishes the sciences and makes them particularly relevant to metaphysics, especially ontology, is their systematic nature. You can learn much by reading *Middlemarch* or *Harry Potter*, or by watching *High Noon* or *Crouching Tiger, Hidden Dragon: Sword of Destiny* on Netflix, much that you would not encounter in a textbook on psychology or biology. Thinking of literature as in competition or incompatible with the sciences would be analogous to thinking of psychology and biology as in competition with one another and with physics and chemistry.

Although I shall often turn to the sciences to illustrate metaphysical themes, nothing I have to say here requires any sort of scientific sophistication. One reason for keeping the sciences in the foreground is that this serves as a reminder that metaphysics resembles the sciences in offering accounts of what there is – not by augmenting or supplanting scientific findings, but by providing placeholders for whatever categories emerge in the course of our most rigorous efforts to get to the bottom of things.

## 1.3  What Now?

If you have been paying attention you will know that this book is meant to be illustrative, not exhaustive. I believe that the best way to introduce metaphysical theses is to do so in the course of developing a coherent overall picture and measuring that picture against the alternatives. I can recall being frustrated as an undergraduate when those instructing us were coy about their own views on particular topics. We knew they *had* views, and we knew these colored what we were told, but we were left in the dark as to when the thumb was or was not on the scale.

I will be guiding you through the territory along a path with many branches leading in different ways to different destinations. I shall, however, do what I can to make it clear what advantages paths not taken might offer, thereby affording you the chance to revisit them later should you be so inclined. Finally, although I am not writing for academic philosophers, I like to think that what I have to say would be acceptable in their sight.

Many of the themes to be addressed might strike you as at odds with common sense. Common sense is a vexed notion, however. Does common sense tell us that Earth is flat, that tables and chairs exist outside our minds, or that things could have been very different than they are? Does Earth appear flat? Well, how would a spherical Earth appear? And how would things appear if nothing existed outside your mind, or if everything were preordained and nothing happened by chance?

You might have views on one or more of these points, but observe that, in the course of taking any sort of a stand on them, you would be engaging in metaphysical reflection. Is it absurd to think that nothing exists outside your own mind? Probably, but why is it absurd? Simply appealing to the appearances here is no help at all, and if you brush off such questions as idle, what are your reasons?

This should give you some idea of what is in store should you stick with me and continue reading. Meanwhile, I propose to illustrate the approach I shall be taking by starting, in chapter 2, with a topic of interest to all of us: the nature of time and its passage.

## Glossary

*A priori, a posteriori*. A subject matter is a priori if it is "prior to" experience, if it does not rely on observation and experiment. Mathematics is a priori. Disciplines that do rely on observation and experiment, empirical disciplines, are said to be *a posteriori*, "posterior to" experience.

*Metametaphysics*. An endeavor aimed at characterizing the subject matter of metaphysics, its methods, principles, and its standing amongst other systematic quests for knowledge.

*Metaphysics*. A philosophical pursuit dedicated to uncovering the most general features of what there is or might be, often in concert with the sciences. Metaphysics includes both a priori and a posteriori elements.

*Ontology*. Metaphysics turned to the discovery and articulation of the most basic categories of being. These serve as placeholders for scientific inventories of what there is.

## Further Readings

Competent introductions to metaphysics that go into more detail on particular topics than I have are widely available. When I have taught metaphysics to the relatively uninitiated, my preferred text has been Keith Campbell's *Metaphysics: An Introduction* (New York: Dickenson, 1976), which, sadly, is long out of print. More adventurous readers might find E. J. Lowe's *A Survey of Metaphysics* (Oxford: Oxford University Press, 2002) penetrating, but at times difficult.

Another out-of-print book by Campbell, *Abstract Particulars* (Oxford: Basil Blackwell, 1990) is eminently thought-provoking and, unlike many more recent monographs, largely non-technical and reader-friendly. Do not be misled by the title. Abstract particulars are not strange rarified entities, but simply properties conceived of in a particular way (see §4.2). Two books of my own, *The Universe as We Find It* (Oxford: Clarendon Press, 2012) and, more recently, *Appearance in Reality* (Oxford: Clarendon Press, 2021) cover many of the topics addressed in the upcoming chapters, but with more attention to detail.

Although I give short shrift here (and elsewhere) to metametaphysics, the collection *Metametaphysics* (Oxford: Oxford University Press, 2009) edited by David Chalmers, David Manley, and Ryan Wasserman would more than compensate interested readers. For a broader metaphilosophical perspective, see Timothy Williamson's *The Philosophy of Philosophy* (Malden, MA: Wiley-Blackwell, 2008).

Finally, the online *Stanford Encyclopedia of*

*Philosophy* (https://plato.stanford.edu) includes entries on virtually every topic discussed here, most of which are commendably accessible, and have extensive bibliographies.

# 2

# Time Goes By – Or Does It?

## 2.0 Yesterday, Today, Tomorrow

The question of how the appearances are related to reality is timeless and universal. Everyone is familiar with cases in which the way things appear differs from the way we know them to be. One example is the moon illusion: a full moon looks larger when the moon is close to the horizon than when it is directly overhead. Or, perhaps most famously, Earth appears to be, but is not, flat. The appearances can be robust. They can persist, even when the truth about them is known.

The moon illusion and the appearance of a flat Earth can be explained, and in that sense resolved. Other cases are more disquieting. The universe appears to be full of things, including us, that persist, move about, and undergo changes over time. Time passes. We entertain thoughts of the past and future, but we find ourselves always in the present, a present always advancing toward the future and away from the past, a "moving present."

If we are always in the present, however, what are we

experiencing when we experience time's passing? Some have found it useful to think of time as a river. You are in a boat drifting downstream. The present is wherever the boat happens to be. What is present now – a willow on the river's bank – will soon be past, replaced by a granite outcropping currently downstream.

> Row, row, row your boat
> gently down the stream,
> merrily, merrily, merrily, merrily,
> life is but a dream

A pleasing metaphor, but one that ultimately proves unhelpful. Consider that granite outcropping downstream. It is there, awaiting your approach. Is this how the future is? Is the future "out there" anticipating the arrival of the present? And what of the willow you passed moments ago? Is the past like that? Does the past persist once you have moved on? In that case, then, given that *you* were there in the past, the past would have to include a past you in a past boat. How would *that* work?

Even if you have ready answers to these questions, you can see that the river of time metaphor is internally incoherent. Were your experience of the passage of time analogous to your experiencing the scene passing before you as you drift downstream, you would be a spectator, not yourself a part of that scene: you are in the boat, not on the riverbank. You, however, the real you, the you reading these words, are very much a part of the passing scene in which we all find ourselves. That puts you on the riverbank, not in the boat, thereby subtracting the element of passage.

## 2.1 The *A* Series and the *B* Series

The river of time implicitly conflates two ways of representing time and its passage that were made salient a century ago by J. M. E. McTaggart (1866–1925) in the course of a discussion of *temporal passage*. Something that occurred yesterday is in the past, an occurrence today is in the present, and an occurrence tomorrow lies in the future. Tomorrow will be, before long, today, and then, some hours later, yesterday. Representing time in this way is to represent time's passing. Yesterday, today, and tomorrow belong to what McTaggart calls the "*A* series."

Suppose you are *here*, and here is San Francisco. St Louis is *there*, to the east. When you travel to St Louis, St Louis is *here*; San Francisco is no longer *here*, but *there* to the west. This is to represent spatial locations *indexically*, that is, by reference to *here*, *here* being wherever *you* happen to be.

The *A* series orders temporal locations indexically by reference to *now*, to the present. If *now* is Tuesday, Monday lies *back there* in the past and Wednesday is *ahead* in the future. When Wednesday comes, Wednesday is in the present, Wednesday is *now*, and Tuesday lies in the past. *Here* and *now* travel with you as you move through space and time.

The *A* series affords a *now*-centered representation of locations in time analogous to *here*-centered representations of locations in space. Spatial locations can be specified without a *here*, however. St Louis is 2,816 km (1,750 miles) east of San Francisco. This is so whether you are in San Francisco or in St Louis, or anywhere else for that matter. Might there be an analogous way of ordering occurrences in time?

Imagine that, on Tuesday, May 19, 2020, you had lunch five hours after you had breakfast and six hours before you sat down for dinner. In putting it this way, you would be locating your actions at intervals along a temporal dimension comparable to your locating St Louis 1,750 miles east of San Francisco. This, McTaggart's "*B* series," is fixed and unchanging. The thought that, on Tuesday, you have lunch after breakfast and before dinner is "eternally" or "timelessly" true: it is true on Monday, and remains true on Tuesday and Wednesday.

McTaggart observed that the *B* series leaves us with a frozen "block" universe. The *B* series admits of no change. For change to occur, for a tomato to ripen and change from green to red, for instance, you need something that is green today and red tomorrow. In a block universe, however, objects do not move through time and undergo changes. Everything is fixed, once and for all.

The same holds for motion: change in spatial location. For that you need something to be *here* – that is, wherever it happens to be – at one time, *there*, and *not* here, at a later time. Motion through both space and through time, then, appear to require the *A* series.

McTaggart argued that anything deserving to be called time would have to include temporal passage, and temporal passage involves the *A* series. Certainly, the *A* series is what comes to mind when we think of our experience of time and its passage. The *A* series is internally inconsistent, however. So, McTaggart concluded, time must be unreal. (Metaphysics in action!)

To appreciate McTaggart's reasoning, focus on the time of a particular occurrence – the moment Neil Armstrong set foot on the moon (July 21, 1969, 2:56 UTC). You, the reader, can say truly that this occurrence is past. For his part, Armstrong, stepping onto the Moon, can say truly of this moment – July 21, 1969, 2:56 UTC – that it is present, and anyone, prior to July 21, 1969, could have said truly that it is in the future. As far as the *A* series is concerned, it is true of this moment that it is past, present, and future! Were time real, were time "out there," *every* moment of time would have to be past, present, and future, and that, McTaggart insisted, makes no sense.

You can see how the argument works by considering a spatial analogue. The *A* series places you in the boat, a spectator on the passing scene as you float down the river. Upstream, the willow is afore (ahead of you), later it is abeam (directly opposite you), and, still later, abaft (behind you). Its being true of the willow that it is ahead, abeam, and abaft reflects the fact that, in describing the willow as ahead, abeam, or abaft, you are not describing features of *the willow*. Subtract *you* from the picture and it would make no sense to say that the willow, or anything else, is ahead, abeam, or abaft.

This leaves us with the B series, which, in effect, places you on the riverbank, adding you to the scene, undermining any sense of temporal passage. The appearance of time's passing must be in us, a *mere* appearance with no foundation in reality. So says McTaggart.

## 2.2 A Fourth Dimension

This talk about the passage of time is all well and good, but if the goal is to understand time, why not ask the experts? Physicists, after all, have had a good deal to say about time. Time, they tell us, is a "spacelike" fourth dimension inextricably bound up with space. The universe is a four-dimensional McTaggartesque block. Its occupants can be at temporal distances from one another analogous to spatial distances. Your passing the willow and subsequently passing a granite outcropping are both there, at a temporal, as well as spatial, distance from one another. You, as you read these words, are really a *stage* or *temporal part* of a you extended in both space and time.

This should remind you of McTaggart's unchanging, B series universe, which lacks the resources to accommodate temporal passage. The passage of time would seem to belong only to the appearances, not to reality.

As McTaggart observed, the thought that things change and objects move from place to place would seem to be at odds with a four-dimensional B series picture. When a tomato ripens, changing from green to red, what you really have are adjacent temporal parts or stages of the tomato. The tomato is analogous to a highway that passes through varied terrain. The highway is shady in some places, bumpy and in need of repair in others. These features of the highway are all there at once. Similarly, one temporal part of the tomato is green, another red. What you do not have is a persisting object that at one time is wholly green and, at a later time, wholly red. The tomato's changing in color is really a matter of its parts – its temporal parts – being differently colored.

In the same vein, despite appearances, when you walk to the store, there is not a single you fully occupying successive regions of space, leaving behind vacated regions. Instead, stages or temporal parts of you occupy adjacent regions of spacetime. Your temporal parts are strictly analogous to your spatial parts. Just as your right half and left half are distinct spatial parts of you, you yesterday, you today, and you tomorrow are portions of a temporally extended you.

Even if you were sanguine about all this – and few are – you might worry about what happens to free will given a four-dimensional universe. We like to think that we control our destinies, at least up to a point: by acting today, you help make tomorrow what it is. But if a later you is merely a part of the same temporally extended entity that includes an earlier you, in what sense could you affect the future, even a little? You could no more bring it about that your future self is one way rather than another than one segment of a broomstick could bring it about that another segment has the character it does.

This idea is so appalling to some philosophers that they regard it as a reason to rewrite physics. If that strikes you as special pleading, ask yourself how it could be rational for you to plan, as you assuredly do, for a future that is no more subject to your influence than the past is.

## Spatial and Temporal Parts

Some philosophers think of spatial and temporal parts as parts of the occupants of space and time. On such a conception, your head and left hand are distinct spatial parts of you. What of your temporal parts? If these were parts of you analogous to your head and hand, you – all of you – would never be anywhere at any given time. The you here now is simply a slender piece of you. Many philosophers reject temporal parts thus conceived.

I prefer to think of spatial and temporal parts differently. Your head and hand are not spatial parts of you, but parts of you that occupy particular regions of space. If you sit down and raise your hand, your head and hand swap their locations. Similarly, a temporal part of you is not a piece of you, but you at any given time.

This way of thinking about spatial and temporal parts can escape notice because we often use locations in space and time to refer to their occupants. When you slice a tomato in half and give me the top half, you are giving me a portion of the tomato that once occupied a spatial region above another spatial region occupied by the bottom half of the tomato.

Analogously, a temporal part of you is not one of a number of parts that make up you; it is you – the whole of you – at any given time.

## 2.3 Going with the Flow

What are the options? Some philosophers, the *presentists*, agree with McTaggart that temporal passage requires the *A* series, but regard this as a feature, not a bug. Only the present is real, the only moments are present moments. The present moment is not something that arrives from the future and recedes into the past. Because the future and past are not on a par with the present, nothing could literally *be* in the past or future, no moment could be past, present, and future, so there is no incoherence.

Anyone who embraced the four-dimensional block

universe would see this kind of response as profoundly inadequate. A proponent of four-dimensionalism could agree with the presentists that McTaggart was right, both in thinking that temporal passage required the *A* series and thinking that the *A* series is internally flawed. McTaggart's mistake was to suppose that, without temporal passage, without the *A* series, nothing is left deserving to be called time. Four-dimensionalists would respond that, what is unreal, what is a mere appearance, is not *time*, but the *passage* of time.

You do not need to be a four-dimensionalist to find temporal passage baffling. If time passes, at what rate does it pass? One second per second? Could time speed up or slow down, or pause, and for how long? If time passes or flows, this would require something for it to flow *through*. A river flows because the water it comprises moves relative to the terrain through which it flows. What would play the part of the terrain in the case of time?

Space, maybe? Aside from worries about the physics of spacetime, this would seem to be at odds with the conviction that space, and its occupants, are themselves *in* time, participants in the flowing. If the terrain flowed with the river, however, in what sense would the river *flow*?

I shall have more to say about the status of time in chapter 7. For the moment – ha! – the discussion will have served its purpose if it has convinced you that the problem of reconciling appearance and reality is inescapable, not something cobbled together by philosophers engaged in unconstrained flights of fancy.

The problem confronts scientists no less than ordinary citizens. Scientists rely on the appearances to build, test, and deploy instruments designed to probe reality. But it is hard to square the universe revealed by those instruments with the appearances. Difficulties we encounter in making sense of the appearance of time's passing and of accommodating this appearance to the physics of spacetime are just two small pieces of a much larger puzzle.

## Glossary

*A series* and *B series*. J. M. E. McTaggart's labels for two ways we have of ordering occurrences in time. The A series is *indexical*, agent-centered. Just as "here" refers to the current spatial location of the speaker, "today" refers to the speaker's temporal location. Yesterday, today, and tomorrow belong to the A series. The B series locates occurrences in relation to one another in time, not relative to the speaker. Unlike something's being here now, something's occurring before, after, or simultaneous with another is eternally true, not indexed to the spatial and temporal location of the speaker.
*Four-dimensionalism*. As used here, the phrase refers to conceptions as "spacelike," a dimension in addition to the three spatial dimensions. An object persisting through time is extended both spatially and temporally.
*Temporal part*. Used here to refer to an object at a time or over a stretch of time. You yesterday, you today, and you tomorrow are temporal parts of you in the way your left half and right half are spatial parts of you. On this conception of temporal parts, objects persisting over time are not made up of temporal parts. Objects' temporal parts are ways of dividing up whole objects analogous to dividing Earth into Southern and Northern hemispheres. Thus conceived, spatial and temporal parts are not to be confused with the material occupants of a spatial region or temporal interval.

## Further Readings

McTaggart's "The Unreality of Time" (*Mind* 17 [1908]: 457–74) introduced the A series and the B series.

McTaggart was inspired by F. H. Bradley's *Appearance and Reality*, which was originally published in 1893. A corrected edition appeared in 1930 (Oxford: Clarendon Press). Neither Bradley nor McTaggart is recommended for beginners.

D. C. Williams' "The Myth of Passage" (*Journal of Philosophy* 48 [1951]: 457–72) contains an accessible and influential discussion of the passage of time. Ambitious readers might look at Theodore Sider's *Four-Dimensionalism: An Ontology of Persistence and Time* (Oxford: Oxford University Press, 2001).

My discussion does not come close to covering the extensive body of work on time. I omit discussion of the distinction between "3-dimensionalism" and "4-dimensionalism," for instance. Katherine Hawley's *How Things Persist* (Oxford: Oxford University Press, 2001) more than fills the gap. Storrs McCall, in *A Model of the Universe* (Oxford: Clarendon Press, 1994), defends an intermediate position according to which the universe is constantly expanding at the "leading edge" along a temporal dimension.

I have omitted, as well, a discussion of time travel. If you are interested, David Lewis's "The Paradoxes of Time Travel," in his *Philosophical Papers*, vol. 2 (Oxford: Oxford University Press, 1986) introduces the subject in an appealing way. Heather Dyke, in "The Metaphysics and Epistemology of Time Travel" (*Think* 3 [2005]: 43–52), provides a compact, reader-friendly discussion.

# 3

# Appearance and Reality

## 3.0 The Saga of Two Tables

Physicist A. S. Eddington (1882–1944) tells his readers that he set out to write his 1927 Gifford Lectures by drawing up, as he put it, "my chairs to my two tables."

> Two tables! Yes; there are duplicates of every object about me – two tables, two chairs, two pens.
>
> One of them has been familiar to me from earliest years. It is a commonplace object of that environment which I call the world. How shall I describe it? It has extension; it is comparatively permanent; it is colored; above all it is substantial.
>
> Table No. 2 is my scientific table. It is a more recent acquaintance and I do not feel so familiar with it. It does not belong to the world previously mentioned – that world which spontaneously appears around me when I open my eyes, though how much of it is objective and how much subjective I do not here consider. It is part of a world which in more devious ways has forced itself on my attention. My scientific table is mostly emptiness. Sparsely scattered in that emptiness are numerous electric charges rushing about

with great speed; but their combined bulk amounts to less than a billionth of the bulk of the table itself. (*The Nature of the Physical World*: ix–x)

Eddington's first table is an unexceptionable occupant of the realm of appearance, the realm in which we go about our everyday business, and scientists go about theirs in their laboratories. The second table belongs to a picture of the universe issuing from those laboratories. The difficulty, remarked by Eddington, is to understand how the two tables are related, and, more generally, how the appearances are related to what science tells us about reality.

One possibility is that the appearances are illusions, serviceable fictions perhaps, but at bottom *mere* appearances. The role of the sciences, and especially physics, is to illuminate the reality lurking behind the appearances. As Eddington puts it: "modern physics has by delicate test and remorseless logic assured me that my second scientific table is the only one which is really there" (1928: xxi).

Another possibility, once popular but less so now, is that physics affords only an instrumentally useful framework for negotiating the appearances, not something to be taken literally. You might be surprised to learn that the philosophers and scientists who promoted this "instrumentalist" conception of the sciences did so on explicitly philosophical grounds. They began with the "empiricist" idea that only assertions capable of observational verification (or falsification) were meaningful. Talk of what was not observable, even in principle, was empty.

Take electrons. Electrons are not themselves observable. Observations of electrons are observations of meter readings or images on computer monitors. When physicists speak of electrons, this is just a convenient way of talking about repeatable patterns of observation. Talk of electrons has no significance beyond these observable patterns. The sciences aim at providing dependable, systematic vehicles facilitating our engagement with our surroundings. One way to accomplish this is to concoct useful fictions such as electrons. These are not meant to depict a deeper reality, but only to guide our systematic investigation of the appearances.

## 3.1 Idealism

If this strikes you as radical or far-fetched, consider its source, Bishop George Berkeley (1685–1753). Berkeley, for whom the city of Berkeley, California is named (although the two are pronounced differently), contended that all that exists are minds and their contents, *ideas*. Ideas were Berkeley's name for conscious perceptual states, what I have been calling observations. All that exists are minds and their contents; there is no external, material world.

Ridiculous, right? Samuel Johnson, a contemporary of Berkeley's, is reputed to have kicked a stone ("with great alacrity") and proclaimed, "thus I refute Berkeley!" *There* is the stone and it is clearly not an idea, clearly *not* something in your (or Johnson's, or anyone else's) mind.

I expect that you are on board with Johnson here, but pause and reflect on what the stone *is*: *describe* it. In describing the stone, you say how it appears: tawny in color, roundish in shape, heavy and solid to the touch. But in offering this description, you are simply describing your perceptions of the stone, appearances. If this is what the stone *is* – and, remember, you were set on describing the *stone* – the stone must be a collection of ideas, appearances, perceptions in your mind and that of others.

Still think this is ridiculous? In that case, you must have good reasons for rejecting Berkeley's assimilation of reality to the appearances. Kicking the stone would be beside the point, as would picking it up and heaving it at Berkeley. All you would be doing is calling up more perceptions (some painful, perhaps). Still, you might insist, there must be something *behind*, and responsible for, the perceptions, a stone *behind* our perceptions of it!

Berkeley is unmoved. What exactly is this stone, the item supposedly "behind" your perceptions? You describe it as before, perhaps adding careful measurements of the stone itself and its whereabouts relative to you. Measurement amounts to your engaging in observable activities on observable objects. So in describing the stone and your measurements, you would be describing appearances, Berkeley's ideas.

Berkeley did not think of this simply as a far-fetched possibility, but as the only game in town. Just as you cannot describe an unperceivable reality "behind" your perceptions, so you cannot so much as entertain thoughts of such a reality. Take the stone. When you describe it, you describe its appearances, how you, and others, would perceive it. If you now proclaim that what you have described is not an appearance, but something behind the appearances, you are speaking nonsense.

Is this simply a clever game, with nothing practical to be said for it? If that is all it is, you should be able to show just where Berkeley goes wrong. And what of those practical consequences? How would your life be any different were Berkeley right? Our practical initiatives are tailored to the world of appearances. Berkeley is not denigrating those, only the further, decidedly metaphysical claim that there is something *behind* the appearances, something that *resembles* them and is responsible for their character. As Berkeley puts it, only an idea could resemble an idea; anything resembling an appearance must itself be an appearance.

If you find such thoughts frustrating, you are in the majority. But, again, it is up to you to find a way of moving beyond them if that is your aim. You could,

of course, simply turn and walk away, but you would
then be in the position of someone who, in failing to
find a flaw in an uncongenial opinion, represses it, and
repression, however artfully accomplished, can be bad
for the soul.

## 3.2 The Reconciliation Project

You might take solace in the thought that, really, if this
is all there is to what I have described as the "problem" of the relation the appearances bear to reality, you
can at least be confident that the psychological risks of
ignoring it are minimal. No one is likely to call your
bluff or think you eccentric. Maybe the appearances *are*
mere illusions and we can leave reality to the physicists.
Or maybe Berkeley was right, only the appearances are
real: life is but a dream. What difference does it make?

As it happens, it does indeed make a difference. It
makes a difference not so much in how we comport
ourselves as we go about our business, but in our appreciation of our standing in the universe. You have already
encountered two time-honored ways of responding to
the difficulty of reconciling the appearances to reality.
The first, perhaps more respectable, option denies the
appearances, relegating them to the status of illusions.
The second takes the opposite view: the appearances *are*
reality; McTaggart and the physicists are not to be taken
literally. They provide, at best, instrumental guidance
that might enable us to cope more effectively with the
appearances.

These two strategies were on display in the discussion of time. Time appears to flow; we are aware of
time passing. What does this awareness amount to?
McTaggart and those who countenance a four-
dimensional universe hold that temporal passage
belongs only to the appearances, not to reality. Time
is spacelike. Your existing over time is at bottom a

matter of your being temporally, as well as spatially, extended. Others, the presentists, for instance, hold the opposite view. Whatever is, is present. The physicist's four-dimensional picture, useful as it might be as a model, is not to be taken at face value.

## 3.3 The Manifest and Scientific Images

Eddington focuses on a troubling disparity between characteristics of experienced objects, on the one hand and, on the other, characteristics we take those objects to have when we reflect on them as a physicist might. The challenge of reconciling the appearances and reality was vividly captured more than a half century ago by Wilfrid Sellars (1912–1989) in the course of distinguishing what Sellars called the manifest and scientific images.

> The philosopher is confronted not by one complex many-dimensional picture, the unity of which, such as it is, he must come to appreciate; but by *two* pictures of essentially the same order of complexity, each of which purports to be a complete picture of man-in-the-world, and which, after separate scrutiny, he must fuse into one vision. Let me refer to these two perspectives, respectively, as the *manifest* and the *scientific* images of man-in-the-world. (*Science, Perception, and Reality*: 5)

The manifest image encompasses the universe as it appears to us – you, and I, as well as scientists working in their laboratories. The scientific image is what those scientists are engaged in spelling out.

Sellars speaks of "fusing" the images and Eddington seems to have something like this in mind when he asks rhetorically: "You speak paradoxically of two worlds. Are they not really two aspects or two interpretations of one and the same world?" His answer: "Yes, no doubt they are ultimately to be identified after some fashion. But the process by which the external world of physics is transformed into a world of familiar acquaintance in human consciousness is outside the scope of physics" (*The Nature of the Physical World*: xiv).

The problem of reconciling the appearances (the manifest image) with reality as revealed by the sciences, especially physics (the scientific image) is both formidable and unavoidable. Even if *you* choose to ignore it, other, more adventurous souls will see it as compelling.

Two approaches to the project are on the table. You might take the scientific image to provide our best guess as to the character of reality, and regard the manifest image as illusory, a kind of fiction, serviceable perhaps, but a veil between us and what there is. Alternatively, you might follow Berkeley and take the manifest image, the world of appearances, as the reality, and the scientific image as another kind of fiction, a finely wrought instrument useful in negotiating the appearances.

## 3.4 Levels of Reality

Is that it? Am I asking you to choose between regarding the appearances as illusory or identifying reality with the appearances? No, I am asking you only to recognize that the problem of coming to terms with the appearances and their relation to reality is forced on us, not by philosophers with too much time on their hands, but by the nature of things. To recognize this is to recognize the inevitability of metaphysics.

Still, it would be regrettable if we were obliged to choose between the two options on offer. Fortunately, other options are available. One of these – suggested, but not in fact embraced, by Eddington – depicts reality as hierarchical: the scientific image concerns a kind of ground floor reality, while the manifest image provides access to "higher-level" realities "grounded" in items belonging to successively more fundamental levels. Eddington's "familiar" Table No. 1 is not reducible to his "scientific" Table No. 2. Both are real. The reality of Table No. 1 is, however, derivative. Table No. 1 depends asymmetrically on Table No. 2. Table No. 1 is "realized by," or "supervenient on" Table No. 2. Table No. 1, the everyday table, is, in this regard, real, but *less fundamental* than Table No. 2, the scientific table.

This hierarchical picture is becoming increasingly influential. Many are convinced that it springs directly from the nature of the sciences. You have physics at the ground floor describing a fundamental reality. Biology describes a less-fundamental, but no less real, reality; psychology investigates a still higher-level reality. You then have the various social sciences – anthropology, sociology, political science – describing realities brought about when groups of individuals congregate and interact. Each level of the hierarchy depends on those at lower levels, but the dependence in question is not *reductive*. You cannot reduce biology to physics, you cannot reduce psychology to biology, nor can you reduce sociology to psychology. The levels are, in this regard, autonomous.

The notion of reduction in play is best understood in explanatory terms. To say that biology is not reducible to physics, for instance, is to say that you could not derive biological truths from truths couched in the vocabulary of physics. A complete description of you and your surroundings centered on quarks, leptons, and fields could not yield truths about your biological or psychological makeup. For that you need biology and psychology. You might be *made up of* quarks and leptons interacting in fields. Take these away and you vanish. But you, and your thoughts and values are something more, something additional. Were this not so, you and your social milieu would be completely captured by physics.

You do not need an elaborate argument to motivate doubts about reduction. Imagine someone's trying to derive truths about your physiology, your tastes in music, your voting preferences, your social circumstances, by

closely examining you at the level of fundamental physics. Again, the idea is not that sociology, psychology,
and biology "float free" of physics, only that they capture distinctive levels of a hierarchical universe. You
could not, for instance, introduce changes at higher
levels without there being changes at lower levels.

If you change your taste in music, this is presumably
underpinned by changes in your body, and those biological changes are in turn underpinned by changes in your
fundamental physical makeup. Because psychology is
not reducible to physics, however, there is no one-to-one
mapping between biological or psychological categories
and physical categories. These "cross-cut." The physical
basis of pain in you might be very different from the
physical basis of pain in an octopus or a Martian.

Philosophers have taken these ideas and turned them
into a metaphysical doctrine: *nonreductive physicalism*. Psychological states that are grounded in, but not
reducible to, physical states are said to be "multiply
realizable." When psychologists and neuroscientists
speak of the brain as being the "substrate" of consciousness, this is what they have in mind.

Hierarchical conceptions of reality have the bases
covered. They show why the various biological, psychological, and social sciences resist reduction, and
they do so without positing "spooky" entities. More
significantly, they neatly reconcile the appearances with
reality, the manifest and scientific images. This is accomplished by rejecting the two-fold appearance–reality
division. You do not have the appearances on the one
hand, and reality on the other; rather you have many
realities, organized in a hierarchy of levels that bottoms
out at a fundamental level, the province of physics.

What could go wrong?

## 3.5 Levels of Difficulty

As even its proponents admit, the hierarchical picture faces a number of difficulties. First, the relation among levels is opaque. What might it mean to say, for instance, that the brain is the substrate of consciousness? Does consciousness "arise from" the brain? If so, where *is* it? Is *it* measurable? Perhaps higher-level phenomena are "emergent" somethings, additions to whatever they emerge from. Emergent phenomena play by their own rules.

Emergence is a difficult topic that I shall set aside for the moment (see §9.3). Here it is enough to note that emergence could be understood as an attempt to salvage the hierarchical conception of reality in the face of persistent, unanswered questions concerning the nature of the connections between lower and higher levels. Meanwhile, we remain largely in the dark as to the nature of those connections.

Setting this difficulty aside, other problems remain. One of these concerns causation and causal powers. Scientists, as well as philosophers, at least since Plato, have regarded causal powers as the "mark of the real": to be is to be capable of entering into causal relations. You can see the point by reflecting on the fact than an entity that lacked causal oomph would be, not merely undetectable, but an entity the presence or absence of which could make absolutely no difference to anything else. How could anyone have a reason to posit such entities?

Carry this thought over to the hierarchical picture. Do higher-level entities have causal powers? Better: do higher-level entities have powers that outstrip those possessed by their lower-level realizers? If they do not, in what sense could they be entities in their own right?

If higher-level entities had their own causal powers, how would these be exercised? It would be odd to think that items at a higher level could have lower-level effects. If they did, this would seem to require "outside" violations of laws governing the lower-level domain, and it is far from clear that we have any evidence of such violations. Still, some proponents of emergence embrace the idea that something is emergent if, and only if, it exerts downward "configurational" forces on its "base."

For many, this is a bridge too far. Perhaps higher-level items have the power to affect and be affected by items at their *own* level of the hierarchy. But again, how is this meant to work? Suppose a higher-level state, your thinking of St Louis, brings about another higher-level state, a desire to visit St Louis. Each of these higher-level states has a lower-level realizer on which it depends. But then, how does one higher-level state bring about another, except by bringing about the other's lower-level realizer? Figure 1 depicts your thinking of St Louis triggering a desire to visit St Louis.

An immediate difficulty concerns the occurrence of your desire to visit St Louis. The hierarchical conception of dependence requires that your desire is realized in some lower-level state, in this case Realizer *B*, most likely a neurological state, a state of your brain. To bring about your desire, then, your original thought would

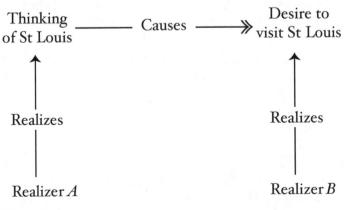

Figure 1

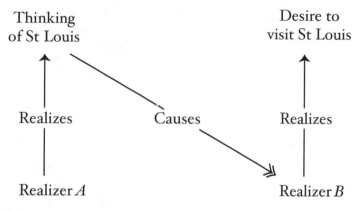

Figure 2

have to cause Realizer $B$, thereby indirectly bringing about your desire (figure 2).

Now the difficulty shifts back to your thought's causing something, Realizer $B$, at a lower level, thereby intervening in the causal milieu to which Realizer $B$ belongs. This would portend the violation of laws governing lower-level processes. In fact, what goes for Realizer $B$ goes for *its* lower-level realizer and, ultimately, some fundamental physical realizer, a dynamic arrangement of fundamental particles, for instance.

For your thought to cause your desire, then, it would need to intervene in the domain encompassed by physics. Such interventions cannot be ruled out a priori, but their occurrence would play havoc with physics as we know it. The upshot would seem to be the situation captured in figure 3.

In figure 3, your thinking of St Louis does not itself cause your desire to visit. Instead, whatever realizes that thought, Realizer $A$, brings about Realizer $B$. Your desire is on the scene, not because of your thought, but because Realizer $B$ is on the scene. And, because higher-level items depend on their realizers, this would have to go all the way down: the causal sequence bottoms out at

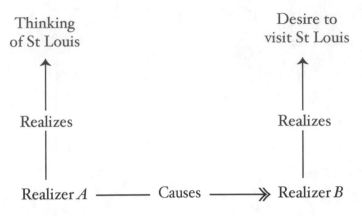

Figure 3

the fundamental physical level. Here, and nowhere else, is where the action is!

This is a straightforward *consequence* of the hierarchical picture, but why imagine that it is in any way objectionable? Recall the thought that causality is the mark of reality. Higher-level items – and presumably there are many levels of such items – apparently have no causal roles. Those roles are filled by fundamental, physical-level realizers. Why, then, think there *are* any higher-level entities?

One reason is that it seems obvious that thoughts, desires, trees, people, brain states, and the like are both real and causally efficacious. Denying that would be at least as radical as going with Berkeley and denying the existence of the material world. There has to be a better way.

## 3.6 The State of Play

Like it or not, once it is pointed out, we, all of us, are faced with the difficulty of reconciling the scientific image, the universe as characterized by physics, with the manifest image, the appearances, the "lived world," as characterized by the special sciences and by our everyday encounters with our surroundings. I have led you through a discussion of three kinds of response to the difficulty.

(1) The manifest image is a fiction; reality is what is encompassed by the scientific image. (Eddington's Table No. 1, the everyday table, is an illusion; only the scientific table, Table No. 2, is real.)
(2) Reality resides with the manifest image; the scientific image is useful instrumentally, but not literally true. (Table No. 2, the scientific table, is a "construct," something invented to enable us to find our way around in a universe comprising familiar everyday objects including Table No. 1.)
(3) The manifest image concerns higher-level, less-than-fundamental realities rooted in a fundamental reality addressed by the scientific image. (The scientific table is a fundamental constituent of the universe; Table No. 1, the everyday table, is a higher-level entity, dependent on, but distinct from, Table No. 2.)

Is this list exhaustive? Each option is hobbled by difficulties its proponents are willing to take on and its opponents regard as deal breakers. Is the only option to step back, take a deep breath, and choose the least objectionable of a sorry lot?

If I had to guess, I would guess that most readers would opt for (3), opt for the hierarchical picture, in hopes that its difficulties could be surmounted and on the grounds that it accommodates both the appearances and the sciences as we have them.

## 3.7 Truthmaking

Before committing yourself and heading for the pub, however, I invite you to consider a fourth option.

(4) The scientific image affords an account of the nature of what the manifest image is an image *of*. (Eddington's Table No. 1 *is* his Table No 2.)

This might be what Eddington has in mind when he speaks of identifying the two tables "after some fashion," before washing his hands of the matter by proclaiming it "outside the scope of physics."

One way to understand this fourth option invokes a conception of *truthmaking*: when something is true, something makes it true. Truthmaking is not difficult to understand. The idea is just that, when a judgment purports to be true of the universe, there must be something about the universe that makes the judgment true. "Here is a gum tree" is made true by the presence of a gum tree in the vicinity of the speaker. "The detector was triggered by a negatively charged particle passing through it" is made true by a negatively charged particle's triggering a detector.

Truthmaking is not a fraught philosophical concept, but something each of us appreciates as soon as we begin thinking about our surroundings. It need not be the case that *every* true judgment has a truthmaker, although it is reasonable to ask, in individual cases, why a particular judgment should be accepted in the absence of a truthmaker. Much more could be said about truthmaking, but I propose to focus on uncontroversial cases such as the two mentioned already and to amend option (4) as follows.

(4*) The scientific image affords an account of the nature of the truthmakers for truths at home in the manifest image. (Eddington's Table no. 2 purports to be an account of the nature of the truthmaker for truths about his everyday Table No. 1.)

Were something like this correct, talk of ordinary tables and their characteristics would be true, not because it concerned higher-level entities, but because states of the universe as characterized by physics fit the bill for tables. You learn, early on, what counts as a table, what does not, and what might or might not count as a table. Our notion of tablehood is not sharp-edged. When the conditions for tablehood are satisfied, it is true that you have a table describable in ordinary terms. But this does not settle the nature of whatever it is that satisfies the conditions for tablehood. Eddington could be right; what you point to, set for dinner, and rest your elbows on is "numerous electric charges rushing about with great speed." Or the truthmaker could be something else entirely. The jury is still out.

You might worry that this would make tables a matter of human convention. Unless there were people on the scene with thoughts about what they call tables, there would be no tables! This misses the point, however. "Table," the word, has a conventional definition, but whatever it is that answers to particular applications of "table" is there whether there is a word for it or not, whether there is anyone about with an interest in tables.

Although I regard this way of thinking about the reconciliation project as promising, I shall be satisfied if I have managed to convince you that there is *something* to the question, how are the appearances related to reality? In that case, you will have accepted that, far from being an idle pastime, metaphysics has a surprising air of inevitability.

## Glossary

*Idealism.* The doctrine that all that exists are minds and their contents. In describing the universe, you are really describing your experiences of the universe. Not only is there no "external world"; the concept of an external world similar to, but independent of our experiences is unintelligible.

*Instrumentalism.* Scientists' appeals to unobservable entities and processes are meant only to assist us in making our way about in the observable universe; they are useful devices not meant to depict any reality lying "behind" the observables.

*Levels of reality.* A conception of the universe as hierarchical: some things are fundamental, other things, dependent on these, occupy successively higher levels. Items at higher levels depend on, but are not reducible to, those at lower levels, the lowest level being the province of physics.

*Manifest and scientific images.* Wilfrid Sellars's names for the universe as it is experienced (the manifest image) and as science, particularly physics, tells us it is (the scientific image). The interesting question is, how might these two images be reconciled?

*Multiple realizability.* The idea that psychological states – and higher-level states, generally – can be realized by very different lower-level physical states. This is thought to be a consequence of the failure of reductionism: higher-level items are not reducible to those at lower levels.

*Nonreductive physicalism.* A metaphysical view according to which everything depends on the fundamental physical makeup of the universe, but the dependence is nonreductive. The dependent things are realized by, or supervenient on, the fundamental things as described by physics.

*Realization.* The relation that higher-level things are

thought to bear to those at lower levels, their *realizers*. Philosophers disagree over what exactly the realization relation is. Psychological states are commonly said to be realized by states of the nervous system, but most of its proponents regard the phenomenon as widespread.

*Reductionism.* In its most strident form, the doctrine that the sciences are all reducible to physics. Biological and psychological properties and laws, for instance, are derivable from laws governing the particles and fields.

*Supervenience.* A term philosophers sometimes use to express the realization relation: higher levels supervene on lower levels. And, as in the case of realization, different philosophers use the term differently.

*Truthmaking.* When a judgment concerning the universe is true, something makes it true. Snow's being white is what makes true that snow is white. The task of uncovering the nature of the truthmakers for truths that have truthmakers falls to the sciences. An account of the nature of snow and its whiteness could be very complicated indeed.

## Further Readings

The chapter's title is borrowed from F. H. Bradley, *Appearance and Reality*, which was originally published in 1893. A corrected edition appeared in 1930 (Oxford: Clarendon Press). Bradley was an important influence on McTaggart's discussion of time, which put in an appearance in chapter 2.

Those interested in the relation metaphysics bears to physics might look at Tim Maudlin's *The Metaphysics Within Physics* (Oxford: Oxford University Press, 2007) and Graham Nerlich, *Einstein's Genie: Spacetime out of the Bottle* (Montreal: Minkowski Institute Press, 2013). Huw Price, in *Time's Arrow and Archimedes' Point: New Directions for the Physics of Time* (Oxford:

Oxford University Press, 1996), looks at the "direction" of time in a pleasingly readable way.

Eddington's discussion of his two tables occurs in the preface of his *The Nature of the Physical World* (New York: The Macmillan Co, 1928). L. Susan Stebbing offers a spirited response to Eddington in *Philosophy and the Physicists* (London: Methuen & Co, 1937; New York: Dover Publications, 1958). Berkeley's *Principles of Human Knowledge* (1710), and, in particular, *Three Dialogues Between Hylas and Philonous* (1713) afford accessible introductions to his defense of idealism. These are available together in a collection edited by Roger Woolhouse (London: Penguin Books, 2004). Wilfrid Sellars's original discussion of the manifest and scientific images, "Philosophy and the Scientific Image of Man," appeared originally in 1962, and was republished in his *Science, Perception, and Reality* (London: Routledge and Kegan Paul, 1963: 1–40).

Problems with the hierarchical, "levels of reality" picture that inspired figures 1, 2, and 3 came to light in the 1990s largely owing to the work of Jaegwon Kim. These are nicely captured in his *Physicalism or Something Near Enough* (Princeton, NJ: Princeton University Press, 2005).

Finally, the significance of truthmaking and ontological seriousness came to the fore in Australia in the 1970s, largely owing to D. M. Armstrong, C. B. Martin, and their colleagues at Sydney University. For recent discussions, see Armstrong's *Truth and Truthmakers* (Cambridge: Cambridge University Press, 2004), Martin's *The Mind in Nature* (Oxford: Oxford University Press, 2007), and chapter 7 of my *From an Ontological Point of View* (Oxford: Clarendon Press, 2003).

# 4

# What There Is

## 4.0 Categories of Being

The remainder of this book takes the inexorability of metaphysics as a given and proceeds to look at issues that arise once you engage with the subject. One characteristic of metaphysical topics is that, considered in isolation, they can appear impossibly remote and otherworldly. I hope to persuade you that this is not so, not by arguing the point, but by example.

This chapter, and the next, are concerned with ontological categories, in the words of D. C. Williams, "the traits necessary to whatever is, in this or any other possible world" (1953/1966: 74). The idea is simple. Ask yourself, what exists? The question is not meant to elicit a motley list that includes, among countless other things, a corkscrew, the number 7, a tree in the quad, the color of ripe tomatoes, the set of black swans, the mass of a particular electron. The question, rather, concerns *kinds* of entity. The corkscrew and the tree in the quad are *objects*. The color of a tomato is a quality or *property* of the tomato, as is its shape.

This gives us two categories, *object* and *property*. A respectable start. But are these categories exhaustive? You might doubt it. Los Angeles is east of Reno, Barack is taller than Boris. Los Angeles stands in a certain relation to Reno as does Barack to Boris. But these relations – to the east of, taller than – seem not to be objects or properties of objects, but something else, something standing *between* objects. So it appears that the original inventory must be supplemented. In addition to objects and their properties, there are relations between (or among) objects.

One way to think about ontological categories is to imagine what an all-powerful God would have to do to create the universe. Would it suffice to create some objects and endow them with properties? It would seem that God would need to do something more, namely *arrange* the objects by placing them in particular spatial – and perhaps temporal – relations.

The universe, then, appears to include, in addition to propertied objects, relations, and to include, as well, *events* and *processes*. Stuff happens. Earth rotates, planets orbit, billiard balls collide, vegetation decays, you grow from an infant to an adult. So, in addition to propertied objects standing in relations, we seem compelled to add events and processes.

What of the number 7 or the set of black swans? These seem to be neither objects nor properties of objects. Are they relations? If you have seven objects, you have a totality answering to the number 7. The objects must be standing in particular relations, but the number 7 does not seem to depend on their standing in *these* relations. If you have any black swans, you have a set of black swans, but, although sets have proved indispensable in mathematics, the *set* of black swans does not seem to be an entity in its own right, not something accompanying the swans as they go about their business.

Such considerations have led some philosophers to assign numbers and sets to a category of *abstract* entities, distinct from mundane *concrete* entities. Abstract entities are not occupants of the universe, but reside in an ethereal realm of their own. Might these be required as truthmakers for mathematical truths? The utility of mathematics would seem to stem from its indispensable role in negotiating the universe, however, not in its holding true of a realm of entities existing nowhere and nowhen. Concrete things here and now are difficult enough to comprehend, so they will be my focus.

## 4.1 Substance and Property

Start with the simplest categories: objects and properties. Philosophical discussions of objects regard objects as belonging to the category of *substance*. A substance is not a stuff, mud stuck to the bottom of your boot, for instance. A substance is a property-bearing entity. A particular tomato in the bin at the supermarket provides a simple illustration. You have the tomato, and you have its properties – its color, its shape – but what are properties?

Earlier I suggested that you think of the tomato's qualities, its redness and sphericality, for instance, as properties. These properties are *ways* the tomato is – the red way, the spherical way. Thus conceived, substance and property are correlative categories: you could not have a substance that is no way at all – a bare substance lacking properties – and you could not have a way that is not a way something is – a property that is not the property of something.

## 4.2 Tropes

This is not uncontroversial. Some philosophers have wanted to dispense with the category of substance, regarding objects as bundles of properties. There is

nothing more to the tomato than its assembled properties. Once you have described the tomato's properties,
you have described the tomato. You do not have the
tomato's properties attached to some mysterious prop-
ertlyless substratum.

The Scottish philosopher David Hume (1711–1776)
was a vocal proponent of this idea, but it has resur-
faced more recently in the guise of *trope theory*. Trope
theorists champion a one-category ontology of tropes,
replacing talk of substances or objects with talk of
"bundles" of tropes. Think of tropes as Lego bricks that
can be put together to form objects. The tomato's redness is a trope, as its sphericality. These, together with
various other tropes, make up a bundle of tropes. This
bundle *is* the tomato. There is nothing more to an object
than its properties: objects are bundles of properties,
bundles of tropes.

Every trope, like every Lego piece, is an individual,
distinct from every other trope. The redness of two
tomatoes are distinct redness tropes. In saying that two
tomatoes *share* a color, or that they have the *same* color,
we mean that they are *similarly* colored. A pile of Lego
pieces that are all the *same* is a pile of similar pieces.
Objects sharing a property is not like our sharing a
pizza, but like our sharing an aversion to cauliflower.
Although they are similar, my aversion is mine, yours
is yours.

Many philosophers have expressed doubts about
tropes as the building blocks – the Lego bricks – of the
universe. A tomato's properties do not seem parts of the
tomato, Lego pieces that make it up. But if properties
are not tropes, what are they?

## 4.3 Universals

One possibility is that properties are *universals*, not
distinct individual Lego bricks. A universal is a repeat-

able general entity, not an individual. When two (or a million) tomatoes *share* a color, when they are *the same* color, this is meant to be taken literally. There is some one thing they have in common. As David Armstrong (1926–2014) puts it, a universal is *wholly present* in each of its instances. The selfsame universal red is wholly present in millions of tomatoes, past and present.

This conception of universals goes by the name "immanent realism": *realism* because it regards universals as real, no-nonsense constituents of the universe; *immanent* because a universal exists in, and only in, its instances. The instances are not *parts* of the universal. A universal is present in its entirety in each instance.

If that is hard to understand, and it is, that might be because you are thinking of particular objects. A material object cannot be wholly present in distinct places at once. But universals are universals, not particulars, a different kind of beast altogether.

Another conception of universals places them alongside numbers and sets outside the spatio-temporal universe. Such a conception is often described as *Platonism*, because it has roots in various of Plato's writings (Plato, *c*. 429–347 BCE). Plato spoke of the *forms*, and these are commonly understood to be universals. This is historically controversial, however, so a better label might be "transcendent realism": *realism* because it accepts the reality of universals; *transcendent* because the universals are not themselves "in" the universe. The universal red, for instance, is not wholly present in the tomato or anywhere else for that matter. Instead, the tomato stands in a special relation to the universal, which remains at arm's length. Its being red stems from its standing in this relation.

Proponents of both immanent and transcendent universals speak of objects' *instantiating* universals, but there is an important difference. Instantiation, in the case of immanent universals, is quite different from instantiation in the case of transcendent universals. The tomato is red. The tomato instantiates the universal red. If universals are *immanent*, then the universal red is present *in* the tomato. If universals are *transcendent*, however, the universal is not present in the tomato, but stands in a distinctive relation to it: the instantiation relation. What might this be?

One possibility is that instantiation is resemblance: A red tomato instantiates the universal red by virtue of *resembling* it (in respect to its color). This might have been how Plato understood the forms. Something is red to the extent that it resembles the archetypal form of red. Were that so, the forms would be *self-exemplifying*: the form of red, would itself be red; the form of the just would be just. I have been following custom, assuming that Plato's forms are transcendent universals, but it is a mystery, at least to me, how something in a shadowy non-spatial, non-temporal realm could be red, or just, or anything else.

Before looking more closely at universals, it is worth noting their part in shoring up the category of substance. If properties are universals (of whatever stripe), they stand in need of *particularizers*. There are many red things, but only one universal red. You cannot build a particular tomato by assembling a bundle of universals. Doing so would yield, if anything, a tomato universal. To account for the fact that universals have many instances – there are many distinct red things – you need individuals that are not universals, but particulars.

This, for proponents of universals, is a job for substances. A substance, unlike a universal, is a one-off, non-repeatable individual entity that provides an anchor for universals. Every tomato is an individual entity that instantiates a variety of properties, properties it shares with many other individual tomatoes: "one over many," one universal, many instances. Were properties universals, this would be possible only with the help of entities belonging to a different category: substances. Without particular, individual, numerically distinct substances, you could not account for the fact that you can have many distinct, individual things that share some or all of their properties.

Substances, so conceived, would be propertyless entities, "bare particulars," *substrata* that join forces with universals to yield individual objects. This idea has struck many as incoherent, or at least deeply mysterious. Trope theory offers an alternative, but the idea that objects were made up of Lego-like tropes seemed wrongheaded. An object's properties do not appear to be detachable *parts* of the object. Are there other, more attractive options?

## 4.4 Historical Interlude

We have tropes and two kinds of universal. Universals can be immanent or transcendent. As if matters were not complicated enough, I shall now inflict on you another conception of properties, one associated with Aristotle (384–322 BCE). These properties resembled tropes in not being universals, but belonged to a two-category, substance–property ontology. Aristotle called these properties *individual accidents*: *individual*, because they are individuals, not universals; *accidents*, because they modified substances "accidentally." A substance can gain or lose accidents, while remaining the same substance. The tomato's being green now is accidental because the tomato will later cease to be green and become red.

The Aristotelian conception of properties as individual accidents was carried through medieval philosophy and informed much of the Early Modern period (roughly, the sixteenth to eighteenth centuries). Prior to the sixteenth century, many philosophers in the West were figures in the Church. Church doctrines offered up a collection of metaphysical puzzles, one of which was posed by the Eucharist. When bread and wine were consecrated in the celebration of the Eucharist, the bread and wine were said to be "converted" into Christ's body and blood. The process was called *transubstantiation*. Christ was said to be wholly present in every drop of consecrated wine and every crumb of consecrated bread. How could *that* work?

Rather than ignoring or sweeping such questions under the rug, medieval philosophers set out to find answers. Think of these topics as metaphysical counterparts of particle colliders in physics. You fed the puzzle into the metaphysics of the day and observed whether what emerged made sense. If it did, this would seem to validate both the theological doctrine and the metaphysics. What might a plausible metaphysical story about transubstantiation look like?

When late medieval philosophers turned their minds to the question, they converged on an interesting picture. Consecrated bread and wine were miraculously "converted" into the body and blood of Christ. But if the bread became Christ's body, then did that mean Christ was bread-shaped, crumbly, and yeasty? And what of the remnants of the bread and wine remaining after consecration? These appear for all the world to *be* bread and wine.

These difficulties were resolved by supposing that, when the bread and wine were consecrated, their *substance* was converted to the body of Christ replete with His complement of divine properties, but – and this is the important move – the properties, the *individual accidents* of the bread and wine, survived, detached from any substances. The accidents could not be accidents of the bread and wine – these were no longer on the scene – nor could they belong to Christ. The survivors were christened "real accidents": *accidents*, because that is what they were; *real* because they were self-standing, existing apart from any substance.

Real accidents are tropes! When the bread is consecrated, Christ is "under" the remnants of the bread, its accidents, which now belonged to no substance.

This did not turn the proponents of real accidents into trope theorists, however. A trope theorist would say that *all there is* to the bread and wine were their respective tropes. There is no underlying substance. Transforming the bread into Christ's body would mean transforming the tropes making up the bread into tropes constituting the body of Christ, and this would not do. The whole point of the exercise was to account for the survival of the bread's accidents, the *appearance* of bread, in the face of a change in the substances to which they once belonged.

Thus, although real accidents might be regarded as worthy precursors of tropes, the serviceability of real accidents required holding on to substances. A real accident begins its career as an ordinary accident, a property of a portion of bread, for instance. Only later, when its substance is replaced, is it liberated.


## 4.5 Modes

Not everyone was comfortable with this metaphysical picture, but, in seventeenth-century Europe, it was risky to question settled Church doctrine. René Descartes (1596–1650), never one to offend authority, suggested in a letter to a reliable friend that there might be metaphysically more elegant ways to handle transubstantiation. (Ironically, this landed him in trouble with the authorities after his death when his letters were published.) Descartes spoke for many when he noted that real accidents were accidents in name only.

Take the bread's whiteness after being consecrated. This was not a whiteness simpliciter, but a white something, and a white something would be a substance: a something that was the white way. Real accidents, in themselves, are Lego-like tropes, but Lego bricks are not properties; they are objects in their own right.

Because accidents had become metaphysically fraught,

Descartes sought a label for properties that would, like individual accidents, be particulars, not universals, but unlike accidents, nondetachable from substances. He elected to follow his scholastic teachers in speaking of properties, not as accidents, but as *modes* (from the Latin, *modus*: *way*).

Modes are modifications of substances, fully particular ways substances are. Ways are not detachable. To be a way is to be a way something is. Think of a bump on the carpet. The bump is a way the carpet is, a way it is configured. You could not subtract the carpet and leave the bump. The bump is not a universal, but a particular configuration requiring something to configure.

If properties are modes – ways things are – it makes no sense to think of them as *components* of substances, tropes. Modes are modifications, not parts. So conceived, substance and property are reciprocal categories. Every way, every modification, must be a way something is, and nothing can fail to be some way or other. The upshot is a substance–property ontology that does not call for universals, exotic general entities. As John Locke (1632–1704), himself a believer in modes, put it: "all things that exist are only particulars" (*An Essay Concerning Human Understanding*: III, iii, §6).

## 4.6 Universals Fight Back

Advocates of universals counter this line of thought by noting that universals provide an explanation for similarities across objects not available to proponents of accidents, tropes, or modes. (To simplify the discussion, I shall henceforth take universals to be *immanent*, wholly present in each of their instances, not *transcendent*, but this does not affect the points at issue.) Two (or a million) tomatoes are similar with respect to their colors because they have a common element, one and the same universal, which universal manages to be wholly present in each individual tomato. Similarity boils down to identity. If tomatoes *sharing* or having *the same* color is literally true, then it is no wonder their colors are similar: everything is similar to itself! If you replace universals with modes, this avenue is not open to you. The color of each tomato is a distinct, individual modification of a distinct individual tomato. Their similarity colorwise is not further explicable.

Is this a problem? Maybe not. Similarity across properties does not obviously call for explanation. If one tomato is red and another is red, they are thereby similar with respect to color. Similarity is an instance of what philosophers call an "internal relation." I shall have more to say about relations presently, but here it suffices to note that an internal relation is one that holds solely in virtue of the things related, the *relata*: if you have those (as they are), you have their being similar.

Even if you thought that that similarity requires no further explanation, a proponent of universals regards this as a draw. Universals have other virtues. Universals can, for instance, explain otherwise inexplicable uniformities characteristic of the universe. Why are there endless numbers of particles with the same properties and the same patterns of behavior? These patterns are captured by laws, and laws seem naturally to call for universals. The sciences are in the business of formulating universally applicable laws. This assumes that similar things must behave similarly, but *why* must they?

The question does not arise if properties shared by objects are literally the same across their instances. If objects with the same mass behave the same way in a gravitational field, this is no cause for wonder. The objects' masses are literally one and the same. You have unity, in the form of universals, amid diversity, in the form of particular numerically distinct substances.

What happens to laws of nature when you abandon universals? Were properties modes, not universals, it would be unsurprising that similar things behave similarly: they are, after all, similar! This is not something that would amount to an unexplained cosmic coincidence in the absence of universals. What might be a cosmic coincidence is that our universe contains just the things it does, and not others. We have electrons, for instance, and not particles, call them electrolls, that are very like electrons, but with a slightly different mass and charge.

I shall have more to say about these matters later, but here I simply note that it is hard to see how an appeal to universals would help. The question, why electrons, and not electrolls, would be replaced by the question, why *these* universals, and not others?

I admit that I have never been comfortable trying to explain universals to the uninitiated because I have never understood what a *general entity* might be. I can say the words "a universal is a general entity, a one that can be wholly present in many times and places at once." I can even give some credence to the claim that universals have some advantages over competitors when it comes to explanation. But always I return to the thought that a universal is a one that can be many places and times at once, and this thought defeats me. The ball's redness is wholly present in this ball, but simultaneously wholly present in myriad other objects, past, present, and future. My understanding of "wholly present here and now" excludes being elsewhere and elsewhen here and now. "Wholly present" seems to mean "present here and nowhere else."

A proponent of universals is free to reply that this is precisely what makes universals special, this is what distinguishes universals from particulars. You could accept this, however, without being any closer to an understanding of what a universal would be. That is where I find myself, and although I do not regard this as providing anything close to an argument against universals, it does afford me with an excuse for not discussing them further.

Before moving ahead, I must issue a warning that, should you decide to delve more deeply into properties, you will discover that there are disagreements among proponents of tropes and among proponents of universals. I have already mentioned two very different conceptions of universals: Platonism (or transcendent realism), according to which universals are *abstracta* subsisting outside space and time, and immanent realism, according to which universals are wholly present in their instances. Still others regard universals as human contrivances existing in the mind and underlying our capacity to classify objects.

As for tropes, most, but not all, trope theorists accept a one-category trope ontology according to which tropes are Lego-like building blocks. Some use "trope" to mean "mode" or "individual accident."

You are likely thinking that all these conceptions of properties, while perhaps important, are confusing and hard to keep straight. You might take some comfort in learning that most philosophers are either oblivious to them or also find them confusing and hard to keep straight. With that in mind, I have included, at the end of this section, a chart that sets out a taxonomy of conceptions of property.

### The Property Zoo

**Properties as universals**
- *Immanent*: shareable, multiply locatable, general entities, wholly present in, and only in, each of their instances; *instantiation* = being wholly present in; an immanent universal cannot exist "uninstantiated." D. M. Armstrong.
- *Transcendent* or *Platonic*: exist eternally "outside" space and time; unlike immanent universals, these *can* exist uninstantiated; instantiation = resemblance? Plato?

**Properties as particulars**
- *Individual accident*: a particularized, non-repeatable, non-shareable quality belonging to some substance, as a particular

way that substance is (see *mode*; *trope, dependent*). Aristotle
and many others.

- *Real accident*: an accident that once belonged to a substance,
  but, as the result of a miracle, now belongs to no substance
  (see *trope, self-standing*). Many, but not all, late medieval
  philosophers.
- *Trope*
  - *Self-standing*: a particularized, non-repeatable, non-sharea-
    ble Lego-like quality; what we regard as objects are bundles
    of individual tropes; much like a *real accident*, but associated
    with a one-category trope ontology. D. C. Williams, Keith
    Campbell.
  - *Dependent*: a particular, non-repeatable, non-shareable
    quality of a substance (see *mode*; *individual accident*); associ-
    ated with a two-category, substance–trope ontology. C. B.
    Martin.
- *Mode*: a particular, non-repeatable, non-shareable qualitative
  modification of a substance (see *individual accident*; *trope,
  dependent*). Suarez, Locke, Descartes, Spinoza.

## 4.7 Substances

In introducing substances and properties, I characterized substances as objects, and appealed to everyday
examples of objects – tomatoes and corkscrews – and
less familiar objects – electrons and fields. All these
are somethings that are various ways, but they exhibit
important differences. Tomatoes and corkscrews are
*complex* objects, objects with parts that are themselves
objects. In contrast, electrons and fields lack parts. They
have spatial (and maybe temporal) parts, but these parts
are not themselves objects.

A conception of properties as modes – modifications
of substances – challenges the idea that property-bearing
substances could be complex. What would a property of
a complex be? You have the simple, propertied parts
duly organized so as to yield, say, a corkscrew. Is the

corkscrew something *in addition* to the particles duly organized? And are the corkscrew's properties ways this additional thing is?

Imagine taking a dozen Lego bricks and assembling them into a cube. You have a cubical complex. This complex seems to have properties its components lack: it is cube-shaped, for instance, but none of its components is cube-shaped. Is being cubical a *property* of the cube?

The cube is not something *in addition to* this arrangement of bricks. If properties are modes, and modes are ways substances are, then the cube's cubical shape would be a way it is, the way the bricks are arranged. More generally, when substances are organized so as to make up a complex object, you do not have a new substance, bearing new properties.

What of the cube's cubicality? It is, after all, the cube that is cubical. The truthmaker for this is this arrangement of bricks: not a property of the arrangement, just the arrangement. The mistake is to think that *words* we use to describe objects must correspond to properties. Sometimes they do, but more often they do not.

Ordinary truths about what we informally treat as properties of a complex object survive unscathed. These truths are not made true by properties of the complex, however, but by the object's constituent substances being arranged as they are. There are properties in the strict sense, and properties in a "loose and popular" sense, *quasi*-properties. In metaphysics, as in most human endeavors, we start with simple cases that are easy to understand but contain the seeds of their own revision.

Suppose this, or something like this, were right. What are the substances? What are the properties? This is not something a philosopher would be in a position to answer. You must turn instead to the sciences. An electron might be a candidate substance, its mass and charge properties. Or the substances might turn out to be fields, or superstrings, or spacetime, or something as yet unimagined.

Ontology is in the business of marking off categories of being that serve as placeholders for the sciences. Although it is hard to imagine a scientific development that would be inconsistent with a substance–property ontology, no philosopher is in a position to rule this out as impossible. Metaphysics does not constrain physics: physics and metaphysics go hand in hand.

## Predicates and Properties

In its simplest form, a *predicate* is a term used to describe – predicate something of – an object. Examples include "is red," "is spherical," "is wise," "is my favourite book." Some philosophers accept a one-to-one correspondence between predicates and properties: whenever a predicate holds true of something, it designates a property of that something.

On this conception of properties – what I called the "loose and popular" conception – if it is true that a tomato is red, this is because the tomato possesses the property of being red. If it is true of a certain book that it is your favorite, this is because the book possesses the property of being your favorite.

Anyone who takes properties seriously would reject this one-to-one, predicate–property correspondence. If properties are modes, for instance, they could be possessed only by substances, and substances are objects that lack parts that are themselves substances. Putting substances together in the right way results in a complex that is not itself a substance, hence not a bearer of properties. Many predicates can hold true of the complex, but not because these predicates correspond to properties.

We would do well to take Bishop Berkeley's advice here and "speak with the vulgar" of properties of complex objects, but "think with the learned," recognizing that "properties" of complex objects are properties in the loose and popular sense: PINO (properties in name only).

## Glossary

*Abstract entity.* An existing something that is not part of the spatio-temporal universe: numbers and sets, for instance.

*Accident* or *individual accident.* For Aristotle, a property, but not a universal, the spherical shape of a particular ball, for instance. Many things are spherical, but their shapes are numerically distinct. The spherical shape of this ball could not have belonged to any other ball. Individual accidents, like modes and unlike real accidents, belong to a substance–property ontology.

*Concrete entity.* Something existing in space and time, including particles, rabbits, planets, and fields.

*Instantiation.* The relation a universal bears to its instances. Spherical things are all instances of the universal sphericality; they all instantiate sphericality.

*Mode.* As with individual accidents, modes belong to a substance–property ontology. Modes are properties but not universals. A mode is a particular modification of a particular substance, a way a substance is.

*Ontological category.* Kinds of entity in the most general sense. Substance, property, and relation are representative ontological categories.

*Property.* A way some substance is, a quality of a substance, the color of a tomato, for instance, or its shape. Some, but not all, philosophers take properties to be universals.

*Real accident.* A property that began life belonging to a particular substance, but has survived the miraculous subtraction of the substance to which it once belonged. Real accidents are integral to accounts of transubstantiation and resemble free-standing tropes.

*Relation.* A property-like ontological category of entities that exist between things, their *relata.* St Louis's being east of San Francisco is a representative spatial relation; your having breakfast before having lunch is an example of a temporal relation.

*Substance*. Something that bears properties that is not itself a property. Traditionally, substances were taken to be entities that do not depend on other entities. A substance can exist in the absence of any other substance.

*Trope*. A property, but not a universal, the color or shape of a particular tomato, for instance. Some philosophers regard tropes as particular ways particular substances are, treating them, in effect, as modes. Most defenders of tropes take tropes to be the building blocks of objects, not unlike real accidents. The tomato's color and shape are parts of the tomato, which is simply an assemblage of tropes.

*Universal*. A universal is a property or relation understood in one of two ways. Immanent realists regard universals as shareable general entities, wholly present in each of their instances. Many objects are spherical, but a single universal – sphericity – is literally shared by them all: a single universal wholly present in every sphere. Others, Platonists, embrace transcendent realism, taking universals to be abstract entities akin to numbers and sets, not present in their instances – or anywhere else.

## Further Readings

D. C. Williams's discussion of ontological categories, "On the Elements of Being," was published in 1953, and republished in a collection of his papers *Principles of Empirical Realism* (Springfield, IL: Charles C. Thomas, 1966). Although he did not invent them, Williams was the first to call tropes, *tropes*; see his aforementioned "Elements of Being." Chapter 5 of my *The Universe As We Find It* (Oxford: Clarendon Press, 2012) includes an account of Williams's use of "trope."

Keith Campbell's *Abstract Particulars*, also mentioned earlier, develops Williams's position in interesting ways, and in addition provides an account of spatial and temporal relations that served as the basis of the one sketched in §5.2. D. M. Armstrong, a colleague of Campbell's at Sydney University, offers an excellent discussion of tropes and universals in *Universals: An Opinionated Introduction* (Boulder, CO: Westview Press, 1989).

Francisco Suárez (1548–1617), in "On the Various Kinds of Distinction" (*Disputationes Metaphysicae, Disputatio* VII. Trans C. Vollert. Milwaukee, WI: Marquette University Press, 1947) distinguishes *modes* from *accidents*, and certainly influenced Descartes' conception of properties as modes.

Readers interested in the metaphysics of transubstantiation might look at my "Cartesian Transubstantiation," which appeared in *Oxford Studies in the Philosophy of Religion*, vol. 6, Jon Kvanvig, ed. (Oxford: Oxford University Press, 2015: 139–57). C. B. Martin's "Substance Substantiated" (*Australasian Journal of Philosophy* 58 [1980]: 3–10) and "On the Need for Properties: The Road to Pythagoreanism and Back" (*Synthese* 112 [1997]: 193–231) are both excellent and accessible. Another paper by Martin, "The Need for Ontology: Some Choices" (*Philosophy* 68 [1993]: 505–22) discusses – and exemplifies – "ontological seriousness."

# 5

# What Else There Is

## 5.0 Relations

What now? Relations have been mentioned as an apt category, in addition to substance and property. Not only are there propertied substances, but there are arrangements of these. In arranging a collection, you organize its components. This is a matter of putting them into various relations. You might put A above B, C to the right of B and to the left of D. Relations hold *between* relata, between A and B, between B and C, and between B and D.

Are relations entities? If they are, they are dependent entities, rather in the way modes are dependent on the substances they modify. Relations depend on their relata: if you take away A, or B, or both, you take away the relation of A's being above B. Still, A's being above B is not *just* A and B. You could have A and B without A's being above B – A might be below or to the right of B, for instance. So the relation looks like something more, something in addition to A and B.

A's being above B is a *spatial* relation as is a tomato's

being one meter from a teacup. As noted in chapter 2, things can also stand in *temporal* relations: an event, your picking up the tomato, might occur before, or after, or at the same time as another event, your pouring tea into your teacup.

Before examining spatial and temporal relations, I propose to consider a case mentioned earlier: two tomatoes being *similar* to one another with respect to their colors (both are red). In what does this relation consist? It would seem to be nothing in addition to each tomato's having just the color it has. If you have two tomatoes, each colored red, you thereby have the one's being similar to the other (with respect to color).

## 5.1 Internal and External Relations

Relations of this kind, *internal* relations, might reasonably be thought to be nothing in addition to their relata. Internal relations would, in this way, be distinguished from *external* relations, which do seem to be something in addition to whatever they relate. Take $A$'s being above $B$. You could have $A$ and $B$ just as they are in themselves, just as they are intrinsically, without its being the case that $A$ is above $B$: you need only rearrange them. The point extends to spatial relations generally. You have the tomato and the teacup without its being the case that they are one meter apart.

What of temporal relations? Are these, like spatial relations, external? Suppose $A$ occurs earlier than $B$. Could this order have been reversed? Could $B$ have preceded $A$? Special Relativity allows that there could be cases in which, from one vantage point $A$ precedes $B$, and from another, this order is reversed. The prospect of time travel seems to allow you to travel back in time and to be present before you were born. Leaving aside Special Relativity and time travel, it is not easy to come up with clear and uncontroversial examples of things *changing* their temporal relations.

In this case, the problem is that once something occurs when it does, you cannot bring it about that *it*, that very occurrence, occurred at a different time. Objects can be rearranged in space, not so for occurrences in time. Even if an occurrence in time cannot be shifted, might it have occurred at a different time? Suppose a particular apple falls from a tree at noon. It could just as well have fallen earlier or later. Yes, but would its falling at 10:00, be *the same* falling? This is threatening to take us into deep waters, so I propose to leave the question of the status of temporal relations open and move on, returning to them in §5.2.

What of other familiar relations? Imagine two stones, one weighing of 11 kg, the other weighing 10 kg. The first stone is heavier than the second. Is the heavier than relation internal or external? All that is required to put them in this relation is for them to have their respective weights. If you have stones with these weights, you have the one's being heavier than the other. The relation is apparently nothing in addition to this.

But wait! You *could* have these stones without the first stone's being heavier than the second. Suppose you hollowed out the heavier stone to bring its weight down to 9 kg. You need more than just the stones to make it the case that the first is heavier than the second, so the heavier than relation must be external after all!

When you compare the stones to determine which is heavier, you are comparing their respective *weights*: 11 kg is greater than 10 kg, and 10 kg is greater than 9 kg. Anything at all with a weight of 10 kg would be lighter than anything else with a weight of 11 kg and heavier than anything weighing 9 kg. So, again, the heavier than relation appears to be internal, not something in addition to the weights.

Once you start thinking seriously about relations, you quickly discover that clear examples of external relations, other than spatial – and maybe temporal – relations, are surprisingly difficult to find. Were *all* relations internal, there would be no need for a category of relations alongside the categories of substance and property. Maybe what we commonly regard as external relations are, on closer inspection, internal relations: if you have the relata, you thereby have the relations. The outliers are spatial and temporal relations.

## 5.2 Spatial (and Temporal) Locations

But *are* spatial and temporal relations outliers? I noted earlier that one object's being above another requires that, in addition to the objects just as they are, one must be situated above the other. Rearrangement is always possible. Suppose an all-powerful God creates two electrons and locates them a meter apart. God could, it seems, have created the very same electrons and located them differently – two meters apart. So the electrons' being a meter apart seems not to be made true by the electrons themselves or their properties, and consequently fails to qualify as an internal relation.

Consider what it is for one electron, $E_0$, to be a meter from another electron, $E_1$. Each electron occupies a spatial location, and these locations are a meter apart. Is a relation between the two *locations* an external relation? Maybe not. If you have these locations, you have their being a meter apart. Locations in space, unlike electrons, cannot be relocated. The relation between the electrons' *locations*, then, is internal. If you have *these* locations, you have their being one meter apart.

Consider a chess analogue. A chessboard comprises an eight-by-eight grid of squares, commonly labeled as in figure 4.

Suppose a knight is on square c6. What makes it the case that square c6 is where *it* is? How could it be otherwise? You might stretch or distort the board in

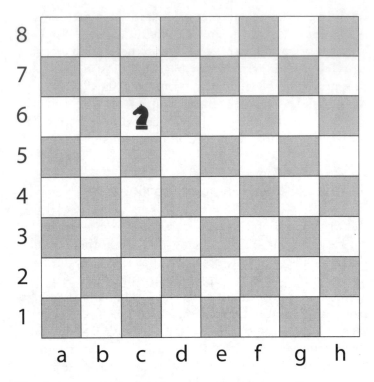

Figure 4

various ways, but the c6 square would remain what it is: the c6 square. What makes the c6 square the c6 square is its location relative to all the other squares. You might swap pieces of wood making up c6 and g6, but that would not amount to swapping c6 and g6.

Return to the two electrons occupying spatial locations one meter apart. The locations' being a meter apart is an internal relation: you could not have these locations without their being a meter apart. Now consider the relation borne by the electrons to their respective *locations*. $E_0$ is at one location in space; $E_1$ is at another. The electrons could have been elsewhere, so their being *where* they happen to be would seem to be an external relation: you could have the electrons and the locations, without the electrons being at these locations. In figure 4, the knight is on square c6, but you could have the knight and c6 without the knight's being on c6: the knight could be on d4, for instance, or e5.

Even if relations among locations in space are internal, then, the relation between a location and its occupant – call this the *at relation* – is apparently external.

Not so fast! Imagine God setting out to create an electron. God does not create the electron, then locate it in space. In creating the electron, God must bring it into existence somewhere (and somewhen); the electron must have *some* location. What makes it the case that the electron is where it is? Well, the electron is wherever it is, and where it is, the electron's location, is just the location it is!

Do not confuse the question, what *brought it about* that the electron is where it is – a causal question – with the question what *makes it true* that the electron is where it is. What makes it true that the electron is where it is, is just the electron's having whatever location it has and that location's being the location it is. What makes it the case that the knight is on c6? The knight is where it is – for it to be in play, it has to be somewhere – and where it is, is c6. Again, the question, what *brought it about* that the knight is on c6, must be distinguished from the question, what *makes it true* that the knight is on c6.

Regions of space have the character of squares on the chessboard. Just as you can move a chess piece from one square to another, but you cannot move the squares, you can move an object from one spatial location to another, but you cannot move the locations. Space might be warped, or folded back on itself, but this would not relocate regions of space.

What of time and temporal locations? As noted in §2.2, physics tells us that time is "spacelike." Were that so, what goes for space would go for time as well. You would not have a three-dimensional universe moving through time; you would have spacetime. Objects would occupy locations in both time and space. These locations would stand in internal relations to one another. Every object has some spatial and some temporal location. Every object is where it is in spacetime. And that location is internally related to every other location. Temporal, as well as spatial relations among objects, would be internal.

## 5.3 Causation

The idea that all relations are internal and, in consequence, not entities in their own right has asserted itself from time to time in the history of philosophy. I shall not try your patience further, however, but simply note that a case can be made for the abandonment of relations as a distinct category of being. The upshot would be an ontology of substance and property. Might there be a need for other categories, however? Earlier I mentioned events and processes. And, come to think of it, what of causal relations, a species of relation not yet considered?

Processes appear to be causally related sequences of events. What of events? The significance of events is linked to causation. When A causes B, A and B are widely presumed to be events, so causation is characterized as a relation among events. Much has been written on the ontology of events, but I shall spare you a rehearsal of the various alternatives, and rely on examples.

One historically influential example of a causal sequence is the striking of a stationary billiard ball by another with the result that the stationary ball is set in motion. Here you have two events: one ball's striking another ball, and the second ball's subsequent rolling. The sequence consists of two events, the first causing the second. An examination of this and similar sequences yields a conception of causation according to which causation is a relation among events that is:

(1) *asymmetrical* (causes precede effects)
(2) *non-reflexive* (no event causes itself)
(3) *transitive* (if *A* causes *B*, and *B* causes *C*, then *A* causes *C*)

Some philosophers, self-styled Humeans, hold that this, together with

(4) whenever an *A*-type event occurs it is accompanied by a *B*-type event (*constant conjunction*)

is *all there is* to causation.

Other philosophers have thought that causation includes a further ingredient. When *A* causes *B*, *A* does not merely *accompany B*, *A brings about* or *necessitates B*. This, they hold, is what distinguishes a mere *succession* of events – just one thing after another – from a causal sequence.

The philosopher Ludwig Wittgenstein (1889–1951) lamented that philosophy suffers from an overreliance on a small number of examples – the use of billiard balls to explicate causation is a case in point. Imagine a ball – a billiard ball, if you like – resting on a cushion. The ball causes a concave impression in the cushion; the ball is responsible for the cushion's being configured in a particular way. But it would be odd to describe the ball's resting on, and thereby making an impression in the cushion, as a sequence. The ball's resting on the cushion and the cushion's being configured are simultaneous. This does not seem to fit the billiard ball model.

Unimpressed? Imagine stirring a spoonful of sugar into a cup of hot tea and the sugar's dissolving. This appears to be a clear case of a bringing about, a clear case of causation. But look more closely. When the sugar dissolves in the tea, the sugar and the tea *work together*, to produce a dissolving. Many philosophers have thought that the sugar and the tea have reciprocal *powers* that, when brought together, yield something new: sweetened tea. Here you have a model of causation that is symmetrical (the sugar and tea work together to produce a certain outcome) and continuous. There is a before and after, but causation is what brings about the transition.

What of the billiard balls? Once again, when you look more closely, you discover that the original description was unperspicuous. One ball approaches and makes contact with the other. The contact is not an instantaneous affair, however. *Both* balls compress and expand with the result that each ball is affected differentially. The interaction between the balls is symmetrical and continuous. So, here, too, it would appear that what you have is, as C. B. Martin (1924–2008) would characterize it, a *mutual manifestation* of *reciprocal powers* – powers inherent in the balls, the table, the gravitational field. These work in concert to yield a particular manifestation.

What if something like this captured an important aspect of causation? Are relations back in the picture? If causation were a relation, how could it be an internal relation? You could, after all, have the sugar and the tea, and the two billiard balls without their causally interacting.

## 5.4 The Causal Matrix

The picture slowly coming into focus is one according to which causation is a kind of *interaction*. Effects are the *manifestations* of powers working together. But what are *powers*? One natural thought is that objects are empowered by their *properties*. A billiard ball's spherical shape empowers the ball to roll. The ball makes a concave impression in a cushion owing to its mass. The identity of a power – what makes a power the power it is – turns on what it is a power *for*. But, with an important class of exceptions, not solely that (for the exceptions, see §5.5). A particular power is the power it is *for* in concert with various reciprocal powers. The ball's sphericality, a property of the ball, equips the ball with many powers: the power to *roll* (in concert with a smooth surface and a gravitational field), for instance, and the power to *make a circular concave impression* (in concert with a cushion).

Brace yourself. I am gearing up to throw an unabashedly philosophical argument at you. First, if objects' powers stem from their properties, given the properties, you have the powers, even if the powers are never exercised. Second, a power's *identity*, what makes it the power it is and not some other power, is its "manifestation profile": how it would manifest itself in concert with various reciprocal powers. The power of sugar to dissolve in a hot liquid and the hot liquid's reciprocal power to dissolve sugar stem from properties of both the sugar and the hot liquid.

Now the punch line. If the identity of a power – its being the power it is – depends on what it is a power for in concert with reciprocal powers, then, if you have the powers on the scene, you have the manifestation. If you did not have the manifestation then, as it were by definition, you would not have *these* powers. Given powers inherent in an ordinary sugar cube, and those inherent in a hot liquid, if the sugar is placed in the liquid, you have these powers being manifested in a particular way: you have the sugar's dissolving.

What about cases in which powers are "blocked," cases in which you have the sugar in the hot liquid but, owing to the addition of a particular chemical, the sugar does not dissolve? In such cases, what you have is not a *failure* of certain reciprocal powers to manifest themselves in characteristic ways, but a *different kind* of manifestation. Sugar together with a hot liquid yield one sort of manifestation; the same sugar and the same liquid supplemented by a particular chemical yield a different kind of manifestation.

If causation is the reciprocal manifesting of powers, then causation is not simply one event followed by another. Causation is a continuous, ongoing, proliferating manifesting of powers. Given an initial arrangement of propertied substances, you have a universe unfolding as it does of necessity, its successive states being manifestations of powers acting in concert and yielding further manifestations. Depending on their circumstances, the substances' powers manifest themselves as they must, yielding a new state of the universe with a new distribution of empowered substances, that in turn yields a new distribution. Everything unfolds as it must from an initial state, if there was one. Bluntly put, if the universe did not unfold as it does, it would not be the universe it is.

## 5.5  Chancy Powers

The resulting picture of a universe of empowered substances evolving of necessity is starkly deterministic. But physics tells us that some things happen "nondeterministically." When a radioactive element decays, nothing causes it to decay. Its decaying is not a manifestation of reciprocal powers. The element has the power to decay spontaneously without the help of reciprocal powers. When you sprinkle in spontaneous manifestings among the others, you introduce an element of chance.

An atom of radium decays at a particular time and, depending on its circumstances when it decays, yields, in concert with those circumstances, a particular outcome. Had it decayed at a different time, under different circumstances, there might have been a very different outcome. Outcomes have downstream consequences, and these have further downstream consequences. If the universe includes genuinely spontaneous occurrences, it could have evolved in many different ways. Its evolving as it has is contingent.

I shall endeavor to clarify these oracular remarks in later chapters. Meanwhile, I note only that none of this requires adding further ontological categories. You have propertied substances distributed in space (or spacetime) and the universe evolving as it does owing to the substances, their properties, and their arrangements.

## Glossary

*Causal matrix*. The complex array of interacting powers that evolves over time as powers manifest themselves in concert with other powers.

*Causation*. As discussed here, causation is a bringing about, the mutual manifesting of powers possessed by objects owing to their properties. Applying rock salt to an icy road causes the ice to melt, but the melting process is symmetrical and continuous: powers belonging to the salt and ice work together so as to yield a melting.

*External* and *internal relations*. An internal relation is nothing in addition to its relata, the similarity relation, for instance: if you have two red apples, you thereby have their being similar with respect to their color. External relations, in contrast, are something in addition to what they relate: you could have the relata just as they are, without their standing in this relation. Spatial and temporal relations are commonly classified as external relations.

*Manifestation*. The upshot of powers working together. Powers possessed by a barley seed, working together with powers inherent in damp soil and sunlight, manifest themselves in a barley sprout.

*Power*. Objects owe their powers – or, as they are often called, their *dispositions* – to their properties. Properties are, in this regard, empowering. A ball has the power to roll owing to its shape. Most powers manifest themselves in concert with other, reciprocal powers. Other powers manifest themselves spontaneously without outside assistance, as in the decay of an unstable element.

## Further Readings

Readers interested in relations might consult two identically titled collections of recent essays on relations: François Clementz and Jean-Maurice Monnoyer, eds., *The Metaphysics of Relations* (Frankfurt: Ontos Verlag, 2015); Anna Marmodoro and David Yates, eds., *The Metaphysics of Relations* (Oxford: Oxford University Press, 2016).

Helen Steward, in "Actions as Processes" (*Philosophical Perspectives* 26 [2012]: 373–88), distinguishes processes from mere sequences of events in a way meant to illuminate the nature of actions – your striking a billiard ball with a billiard cue, for instance.

C. B. Martin was an early champion of the idea that objects' properties were empowering: interactions among objects are a matter of the mutual manifestation of the objects' reciprocal powers. This is importantly different from the view that properties *are* powers. Martin's properties are qualities that empower their possessors in various ways with various reciprocal partners. His "Dispositions and Conditionals" (*Philosophical Quarterly* 44 [1994]: 1–8), which had been written and presented at conferences more than 30 years earlier, is both important and accessible. The notion of a causal matrix stems from Martin's "power nets." This is spelled out in some detail in Martin's *The Mind in Nature* (Oxford: Oxford University Press, 2007).

# 6

# One from Many, Many from One

## 6.0 Essences

If ever there were a rarified metaphysical topic it would be essences. The history of philosophy abounds in discussions of essences and essential properties. But what are essences, and why should anyone care about them? Once again, I ask for your patience while I wax philosophical. The discussion will return to earth soon enough.

According to Bishop Joseph Butler (1692–1752), "every thing is what it is and not another thing." Brilliant! How could it be otherwise? The apparent triviality of Butler's remark masks its deeper significance, however.

Phar Lap is a horse. A fancy way to put this invokes essences: Phar Lap has the "essence of horsehood." You have a grasp of Phar Lap's essence if you know *what it is to be a horse*, and recognize, if only dimly, that Phar Lap *has what it takes to be a horse*. Knowing the essence of a horse is to know what it is to be a horse – rather than a donkey or a kangaroo. Your grasp of an essence can come in degrees. You can know well enough what a horse is, without knowing what Aristotle called the "real definition" of a horse. Think of a real definition as an exhaustive specification of the requirements for horsehood.

Some philosophers have understood essences as *entities*, the role of which is to *bring it about* that something is a horse, or a donkey, or a kangaroo, or a water molecule. Here it is well to keep in mind a distinction introduced in §5.2. When you wonder what makes it the case that Phar Lap is a horse, you might have in mind either

(1) what *brought it about* that Phar Lap is a horse, or
(2) what *makes it true* that Phar Lap is a horse.

If you take Phar Lap's essence to be what brings it about that Phar Lap is a horse, you are thinking of essences as causal factors. Some credit Aristotle with this idea, and Locke might have had something like this in mind in speaking of "real essences," describing these as "the real internal, but generally in Substances, unknown Constitution of Things, whereon their discoverable Qualities depend" (*An Essay Concerning Human Understanding*: III, iii, §15).

You can get a feel for essences thus conceived by considering a familiar liquid, water. Water is largely made up of $H_2O$ molecules, so you might regard $H_2O$ as the essence of water. What of Phar Lap? Perhaps Phar Lap's essence is his DNA. Phar Lap's DNA includes instructions for building a horse. Horses, and only horses, have such DNA. Thus, a case could be made for saying that Phar Lap's DNA is *both* what brings it about that Phar Lap is a horse *and* what makes it true that he is a horse.

Certainly, it is the case, at least as an approximation, that water is made up of $H_2O$ and that horses, and only horses, have equine DNA. There is, however, another, rather different, conception of essences, one that comes closer to catching the deeper significance of Bishop Butler's adage. "*Every* thing," Butler says, "is what it is." In the sense in which this is true, it is true of necessity. Butler's target is not classes or kinds of thing, not the species horse, not water generally, but individual things of whatever sort.

Imagine picking up a particular billiard ball. The billiard ball, like anything else, is what it is. But *what* is it? Perhaps it is a cloud of particles or a concentration of energy in a field. As it happens the cloud of particles, or energy concentration, could have what it takes to be a billiard ball. This (pointing to the billiard ball) has what it takes to be a cloud of particles, and this cloud has what it takes to be a billiard ball. More than that, it has what it takes to be a red sphere, a sphere, something with a mass of .16 kg, and much else besides.

Billiard balls, horses, and quantities of water are more or less self-contained, but consider a fanciful philosopher's "object" made up of Grant's tomb, a pebble on the surface of the Moon, and a golf ball at the bottom of a pond in St Andrews. The object is hokey and gerrymandered, but no less real for that. It has what it takes to be what it is, it has, as every thing has, an essence. To be sure, what *it* is is supremely uninteresting, but that is irrelevant to its being what it is. You could, if you liked, give it a name, Bruce.

## 6.1 Wholes from Parts

Where is this leading? One high-profile metaphysical issue today centers on the "special composition question": when do composites made up of parts qualify as genuine wholes? When do objects – the particles, say – count as parts of something, some one thing?

Some philosophers, the *nihilists*, hold that there are *no* composite objects. All that exists are simples, particles, distributed in space and time. What we call a billiard ball is not a unity, a whole made up of atoms, its parts, but an array of particles rather like a dense cloud shaped in a particular way that answers to the label "billiard ball." The collection has no language-independent standing. If no one were around to single out and label collections resembling this one, there would be no billiard balls.

Other philosophers, the *universalists*, take the opposite view: *any* collection counts as an object. Bruce, then would be a perfectly respectable object alongside Phar Lap, a water molecule, and the billiard ball.

Still other philosophers defend explicit answers to the special composition question, offering a principled way of distinguishing the sheep – genuine objects – from the goats – gerrymandered, non-objects, mere collections with no intrinsic unity. One such philosopher, Peter van Inwagen, the source of contemporary interest in the special composition question, holds that all that exists are the particles – the simples – and living things.

Why living things? A living thing has an internal source of unity that admits the addition, replacement, and subtraction of the simples that make it up, while retaining its identity. The particles that make you up are constantly coming and going. It is more than likely that the particles that made you up when you were five years old were completely replaced by the time you reached age ten. Nevertheless, there is just the one you. The you at five, the you at ten, and the you now are a single you.

This is not so for Bruce. Bruce has no inner unity. Bruce's unity stems, not from Bruce, but from our decision to count a collection of three things as a one. If you remove the golf ball, leaving only Grant's tomb and a lunar pebble, or replace the golf ball with a different golf ball, Bruce is no more.

According to van Inwagen, only living things afford the right kind of natural unity, only living things qualify as genuine wholes with parts. Other philosophers have offered broader principles designed to admit artefacts and objects we commonly take to be objects, inorganic molecules, for instance, and billiard balls, alongside living things, as genuine objects with parts. The difficulty is to come up with a principled way to distinguish the real objects from the pretenders. Try it! You will quickly discover that principles that yield the answer you seek for some cases either exclude other candidate objects or admit what seem clearly to be non-objects – Bruce, for instance.

## 6.2 Complexes and Their Parts

You might be inclined to take this as evidence that talk of essences and attempts to answer the special composition question are a waste of time, time that could be better spent playing *Fortnite* or sleeping. Bear with me and return to a conception of the universe as a vast collection of particles, many interacting and transforming others and being transformed in turn – as in the case of particles collected together in an atom, or a molecule, or a living cell. Everything in the universe is what it is, everything has what it takes to be whatever it is, each particle, each collection of particles, however intimately bonded together or loose and separate, as with Bruce.

No collection is "better," "more real," or more or less "fundamental" than any other. As it happens, some collections attract attention, perhaps because many other collections have what it takes to be collections of that kind. When this is so, our practice is to introduce a word designed to refer to collections that have what it takes to be collections of that sort. "Horse," "water molecule," "billiard ball" are obvious examples. Bruce, in contrast, is a one-off, beneath consideration.

Collections that arise naturally constitute what are commonly called *natural kinds*, provided only that they are reasonably plentiful. Horses and water molecules would seem to qualify. Their essences are shared by many similar instances: many things have what it takes to be horses, and many more things have what it takes to be water molecules. Often these collections feature objects with reciprocal powers that work together so as to insure a measure of cohesion and stability. If similar objects are similarly empowered, it would be possible to formulate laws that capture the interplay of powers – within and among complexes.

This, at any rate, is how things would be, were the universe to consist of empowered particles distributed across space and time, the starting point for philosophers bent on articulating a principled answer to the special composition question. One lesson is that, whatever essences are, they are not a kind of entity. It might be that in order to have what it takes to be a horse, Phar Lap must have equine DNA, and it might be that to have what it takes to be a quantity of water, a liquid must consist largely of $H_2O$ molecules. But the DNA and the molecules are not themselves essences. The essence of a horse is what it is to be a horse, or, as I prefer, what it takes to be a horse, and that is not an entity.

## 6.3 Identity and Composition

A second lesson is that essences, not being entities, are not active players, not metaphysical workhorses. Their utility consists in providing a way to move beyond metaphysical puzzles that are almost exclusively the province of philosophers. One of these is the special composition question. Another concerns the possibility of coinciding objects.

Take a deep breath and consider, on the one hand, the Statue of Liberty, and, on the other hand, the quantity of copper that makes up the statue. How many objects are present? You might think there is just one object, a statue-shaped quantity of copper that goes by the name, Statue of Liberty. But consider: the statue could continue to exist in the absence of the quantity of copper – were the copper replaced gradually in the course of repairing the statue over many years. Similarly, were the statue melted down, the quantity of copper could survive in the absence of the statue.

Statues and quantities of copper evidently have different essences, hence different *identity* and *persistence conditions*. The same statue over time might not consist in the same quantity of copper, and the same quantity of copper over time might not make up the same statue. Put in terms of essences, the essence of a quantity of copper and the essence of a statue are importantly different. What it takes to be a particular quantity of copper is not what it takes to be a particular statue. Statues and quantities of copper are different kinds of object. This has suggested to some that, in the case of statues, you have *coinciding objects*: the statue and the quantity of copper that makes it up.

### Essence and Identity

A rabbit's *essence* is what it is to be a rabbit, what it takes to be a rabbit. You could call this a *general essence*.

Bunkin, the rabbit, in addition to having what it takes to be a rabbit, has what it takes to be Bunkin, this individual rabbit. This is Bunkin's *individual essence*.

Knowing a rabbit's essence includes knowing how to *individuate* rabbits, knowing what distinguishes rabbits from other things. It includes, as well, knowing *criteria of identity* and the *persistence conditions* for rabbits, knowing how to *count* rabbits, knowing what makes it the case that the rabbit in your garden today is, or is not, the *same* rabbit that was in your garden yesterday.

Similar arguments have been advanced to show that you and your body must be distinct. You could survive dramatic bodily alterations and perhaps even the complete demise of your body – if, as science fiction would have it, you could be programmed into another's brain, for instance. Similarly, your body could survive your absence were you placed in a persisting vegetative state. Although you currently coincide with your body, you are not your body, just as the statue is not the quantity of copper with which it, for a time, coincides.

Discussions of this kind invoke the concept of *identity*. Identity is another of those concepts the simplicity of which makes them awkward to discuss. One place to start is by distinguishing cases in which *A* is identical *to* (that is, exactly similar to) *B*, from those in which *A* is identical *with B*, *A is B*, "*A*" and "*B*" are two ways of referring to one and the same. Judy is identical *to*, not *with*, her twin sister, Trudy. In contrast, the Morning Star is identical *with* the Evening Star. The Morning Star *is* the Evening Star; the "Morning Star" and the "Evening Star" are names for one and the same heavenly body. To be sure, if the Morning Star and the Evening Star are one and the same, then the one must be identical *to* the other. This is just to say that everything is identical *with*, hence *to* itself.

Now recall the statue and the quantity of copper, and you and your body. Is the statue identical with the quantity of copper that makes it up? Are you identical with your body? Well, if *A* is identical with *B*, if *A is B*, everything true of *A* must be true of *B*, and vice versa. If the Morning Star is identical with the Evening Star, then if the Morning Star is bright, the Evening Star must also be bright. If the mass of the Morning Star is $4.867 \times 10^{24}$ kg, the mass of the Evening Star must also be $4.867 \times 10^{24}$ kg. (It is probably time to admit that the Morning Star and the Evening Star are traditional names for the selfsame heavenly body, *Venus*.)

In contrast to the Morning Star and the Evening Star, there are many things true of the quantity of copper that are not true of the statue (and vice versa). The copper could survive momentous changes in shape that the statue could not: if the copper is melted down into a large spherical block, for instance, the copper remains, but the statue goes out of existence. The reverse is true as well. The statue could survive changes that the copper could not. Similarly, in the case of you and your body, your body could undergo changes that you could not, and vice versa.

It would seem to follow that the statue and the copper of which it is made are distinct objects, and that although you and your body might coincide, at least for a time, you are not your body. The slogan: composition is not identity. The statue is *composed* of a quantity of copper, but is not *identical with* the copper that makes it up. You are *composed* of flesh and blood, but you are not – not *identical with* – that flesh and blood.

## 6.4 Essences to the Rescue

This has the sound of an important, if puzzling discovery. Where we thought there was just one object, there are two that happen, for a time at least, to coincide. One immediately obvious worry is that, if the quantity of copper has a mass of 150,000 kg, and the statue has a mass of 150,000 kg, then if they are distinct objects, the two together must, it would seem, have a mass of 300,000 kg, but they do not. Perhaps the statue and the lump share some properties and not others. But, if properties are modifications of objects, modes, how could distinct objects share a property?

This is simply one of many problems raised by the prospect of coinciding objects. I have selected it because it nicely illustrates one of the running themes of this book. Metaphysics cannot be done piecemeal. The discussion of properties in chapter 3 has direct application to questions about identity. My hope is that you will come to appreciate the extent to which metaphysical issues are intertwined, and no less intertwined with the sciences and with everyday concerns.

Frustrated? Who could blame you? But before tossing

this book aside, reflect one last time on essences as I have characterized them. A statue's essence differs from the essence of a quantity of copper. This is just to say that what it takes to be a statue is different from what it takes to be a quantity of copper. Similarly, your essence differs from that of your body: what it takes to be a body differs from what it takes to be a person.

The supposition in play is that a quantity of copper and a human body are clouds of particles. One and the same cloud could have what it takes to be a quantity of copper, and, for a time, also have what it takes to be a statue. In the same way, the cloud, or a succession of clouds, of particles that has what it takes to be a human body could, for a time, have what it takes to be a person.

Given the ubiquity of essences, given that everything, from the outlandish to the commonplace, is what it is, everything has an essence. Some of these things are relatively compact and stable, others are not. We invent names for those that stand out and exhibit similarities, hence uniformities in behavior, with others but these are in no sense privileged.

Does this go too far? Does this turn horses, billiard balls, persons, and planets into mere constructs, human inventions? If the boundaries we draw reflect our own interests and limitations, they would be, from the impersonal perspective of the universe, arbitrary, even, in some cases, whimsical.

This would be the wrong lesson to draw, however. Remember Bruce, the hokey object consisting of Grant's Tomb, a pebble on the surface of the Moon, and a golf ball at the bottom of a Scottish pond introduced in §6.1? Is Bruce an invention, did I create Bruce? How could I have done? I created the name, perhaps, but I did not create Bruce. Bruce is there quite independently of me or anyone else. So it is with our other cases. The fact that we single out certain objects and shun others does not create those objects. They would be there whether anyone bothered to single them out or not.

## 6.5 Parts from Wholes

Philosophers who engage with these issues do so with a certain picture of the universe in mind. I have been playing along with this picture because I am doubtful whether, in its absence, anything very exciting would survive. The picture in question is atomistic: the universe comprises simple, partless "atoms" that move about, enter into arrangements as their natures and trajectories allow.

The imagined atoms are not what we call atoms today, but closer to what the ancient Greeks – Epicurus (341–270 BCE), for instance – called atoms. Atoms as we now conceive them are themselves built up from parts – electrons, protons, and neutrons – and protons and neutrons in turn are made up of quarks. Philosophers' atoms are idealizations deployed as a matter of illustration. You have a universe with simple, partless substances, and collections of these. The question then becomes, which collections amount to objects, which do not?

For all we know, however, the universe does not have this granular, atomistic character. For all we know, the universe comprises continuous somethings, the fields, perhaps, or a single unified field, or spacetime. Were that so, what we regard as distinguishable objects would be smears or energy concentrations in fields, or wrinkles in spacetime. Atoms, whether atoms as we currently conceive of them or Epicurean atoms, would not be substances, but properties, modifications of some substance or substances. I shall have more to say about this possibility later; at present I want only to consider its implications for the special composition question and putatively coinciding objects.

In a seamless universe, parts would be parts in name only – a modification of something is not a part of that something. Objects, ultimately substances, play host to modifications. Were the universe to have a seamless character, the question would be, what kinds of modification correspond to what we regard as objects: electrons, molecules, tomatoes, billiard balls. Given the absence of parts, there would be no natural unities in which parts conspire to make up wholes. Parts, not wholes, would be at risk!

What of coinciding objects? Again, the objects at issue would belong, not to the category of substance, but to the category of property. They would be modifications of some host, and the question would be, could you have coinciding modifications? Yes and no. You might think a billiard ball's shape and color coincide. These are distinct but coincident modifications of the ball. But, to return to an earlier example, if a statue and a quantity of copper coincide, both the statue and the quantity of copper have a shape. Could two *shapes* coincide?

A conception of essences as *what it is to be* affords an answer. One and the same configuration of particles or distribution of energy in a field could serve as truth-maker for "this is a statue" and for "this is a quantity of copper." Insisting that distinct truths call for distinct objects, distinct truthmakers, only invites confusion, a kind of confusion characteristic of many philosophical puzzles.

I have taken you on a detour through imagined seamless, partless universes to call attention to the role played by a seemingly innocent starting point – in this case atomism – in generating a philosophical problem. Atomism is an empirically tinged starting point, that, so far as anyone knows, could prove to be off base.

This is not empty philosophical hand waving. The conception of the universe as continuous comes from physics, although it has existed in various guises from the dawn of science and from the days when scientists called themselves natural philosophers. Metaphysics does not constrain science. On the contrary, a viable metaphysics must be able to accommodate whatever the sciences throw at it.

## 6.6 Personal Identity

Before moving on, one topic that put in a brief appearance in §6.3 deserves mention. In discussing identity
and persistence, I observed that persistence and identity
conditions apparently differ for you and your body. This
suggests that, whatever *you* are, you are not to be identified with your body. You at age five and you at age
ten are the same you, despite endless changes in your
body. But what exactly are your identity and persistence
conditions? You are a person, but what is it to be a
person – as opposed, say, to a human body? This is the
problem of *personal identity*: what does it take to be a
person, and what makes you now, you as a ten-year-old,
and you as a five-year-old the same person?

An adequate discussion of answers to these questions
would require – at least – a very large book. Competing
answers offer competing accounts of the essence of
personhood. Some argue that persons *are* their bodies.
Others think of bodies as vessels for persons. Perhaps
persons are programs running on neural computers,
or nonmaterial souls attached to, but independent of,
bodies.

According to Locke, a person is "a thinking intel-
ligent being, that has reason and reflection, and can
consider itself as itself, the same thinking thing, in different times and places." You, as a five-year-old, entertain
thoughts and undergo experiences that you later recall
as a ten-year-old and regard as yours. Now, even if your
memories of thoughts and experiences you had as a five-
year-old are hazy, you recall having earlier thoughts and
experiences and the thinker of those thoughts recalls
having earlier thoughts that belonged to a still earlier
thinker. In this way, you are connected to all those past
yous.

Various versions of this "psychological continuity"
account of the identity and persistence conditions for

personhood have been defended, refined, and attacked. The ongoing debate has produced a trove of entertaining thought experiments. One of these involves "fission." Suppose, as a result of a catastrophic accident you undergo a brain operation in which the two hemispheres of your brain are separated. These are then transplanted inside the heads of two patients in need of a brain transplant. When these patients awake from surgery, each will have thoughts and memories that are continuous with yours prior to the accident. Which (if either) one is *you*? Or are there now *two* yous?

The question of personal identity is a question as to the essence of personhood, what it takes to be a person. A grasp of the essence would equip you, to the extent that it is possible, to deploy identity and persistence conditions for persons. So what *is* the essence, what *is* it, *what does it take*, to be a person? My suspicion is that our sense of what it is to be a person is neither univocal or sharp-edged. It varies across medical, psychological, legal, political, religious, and many other domains. One person, one vote, for instance, calls on aspects of personhood that differ from those of the psychiatrists and neurosurgeons.

There are undoubtedly important similarities across these, and perhaps even a central core shared by all of them. What seems unlikely is that there is a kind of entity "out there," independent of our various interests, waiting to be discovered by philosophers. This does not mean that it is pointless to talk of persons, or that there really are no persons, or that persons are a human contrivance. Particular human beings can have what it takes to be persons for purposes of voting or census taking, for instance. We invented the criteria for what counts as a person in such cases, but we did not invent the beings who satisfy it.

I am probably in the minority on this matter, but my aim has not been to spell out and defend a position on the identity of persons, the essence of personhood, but only to introduce you to a metaphysical topic. I leave it to you to explore the alternatives and find one you are comfortable with *and* that comports with your opinions on the other topics addressed in this book. If the topic piques your curiosity, however, I encourage you to follow it up. A good starting place would be the readings set out at the end of the chapter.

## Glossary

*Essence.* As used here, an entity's essence is *what it is to be* an entity of the kind it is. So regarded, essences are not themselves entities. The essence of a horse is what it takes to be a horse, what makes it true that something is a horse. Some philosophers do regard essences as entities, the essence of a horse being something in a horse that brings it about that the horse is a horse, and not something else.

*Identity* and *persistence* conditions. Knowing the essence of a wallaby includes knowing how to count wallabies, knowing what distinguishes one wallaby from another, and knowing what would make it true that this wallaby is, or is not, the wallaby you spotted yesterday.

*Individuation.* If you know the essence of something, a wallaby, say, you know how to individuate wallabies, how to distinguish wallabies from things that are not wallabies.

*Personal identity.* Accounts of personal identity endeavor to capture the essence of personhood: what it takes to be a person, what distinguishes one person from another, and what would make it true that the person you pass on the street today is, or is not, the same person and the one you walked past last week.

*Real definition.* Expresses an essence. To know the real definition of water, for instance, is to know what it takes to be water.

*Special composition question.* When do composite

entities made up of parts count as genuine wholes? Nihilists answer, never: there are no privileged wholes, only simples standing in various relations to one another. Universalists, take the opposite tack, holding that any collection of simples, however widely dispersed, are genuine wholes. Both nihilists and universalists agree that we care about some collections more than others, but there is no mind-independent principle of unity that sets off some wholes from others. Others argue that some collections, living things, for instance, qualify as genuine wholes, some do not.

## Further Readings

Bishop Butler ("every thing is what it is and not another thing") is often misquoted as "everything is what it is and not another thing." The comment appears in the preface to his *Fifteen Sermons Preached at Rolls Chapel* (London: J. and J. Knapton, 2nd edn, 1729).

My discussion of essences owes much to E. J. Lowe; see, for instance, his "Metaphysics as the Science of Essence," which was published posthumously in A. D. Carruth, S. C. Gibb, J. Heil, eds., *Ontology, Modality, and Mind: Themes from the Metaphysics of E. J. Lowe* (Oxford: Oxford University Press, 2018: 14–34). Saul Kripke's *Naming and Necessity* (Cambridge, MA: Harvard University Press, 1980), provides an elegant and influential discussion of essences inspired by Locke's.

More recently, Kit Fine has advanced an account of essence closer to Lowe's. See his "Essence and Modality" in a collection edited by James Tomberlin, *Logic and Language* (*Philosophical Perspectives*, vol 8. Atascadero, CA: Ridgeview Press, 1994: 1–16), and "Coincidence and Form" (*Proceedings of the Aristotelian Society* Supp. 82 [2008]: 101–18). Works by Katherine Koslicki and Simon Evnine, cited as suggested readings for chapter 7, would also be relevant.

Current discussion of parts, wholes, and the special composition question is rooted in Peter van Inwagen's *Material Beings* (Ithaca, NY: Cornell University Press, 1990). The literature is vast, but the essays in *Composition is Identity*, edited by A. J. Cotnoir and D. L. M. Baxter (Oxford: Oxford University Press, 2014) would give you a feel for the territory.

Although I did not go deeply into the topic of personal identity, many others have. The anchor is Locke's discussion in book 2, chapter 27 of the 2nd (1694) edition of his *Essay on Human Understanding* (Peter Nidditch, ed., Oxford: Clarendon Press, 1975). Derek Parfit's *Reasons and Persons* (Oxford: Oxford University Press, 1984) is a modern classic. E. J. Lowe's *Subjects of Experience* (Cambridge: Cambridge University Press, 1996) provides an account of persons that stands apart. Lowe is a contributor to *Personal Identity: Simple or Complex?*, edited by Georg Gasser and Matthias Stefan (Cambridge: Cambridge University Press, 2012). Another important collection, edited by Peter van Inwagen and Dean Zimmerman, *Persons: Human and Divine* (Oxford: Oxford University Press, 2007), includes essays on both human and heavenly persons.

# 7

# Aristotle vs Hume

## 7.0 Bringings About

The discussion of causation in §§5.3–5.4 developed a conception of causation according to which causal relations are necessitatings or, better, *bringings about*. When billiard balls collide, they interact so that each ball's trajectory is altered. When you stir sugar into hot tea, the tea and the sugar interact, with the result being sweetened tea.

A conception of this kind depicts the universe as a distribution of objects ranging from the very small to the very large, from electrons, to molecules, to rabbits, tables and chairs, to planets, stars, and black holes. Objects have properties that empower them in various ways in concert with reciprocally empowered fellow objects.

The manifesting of powers is symmetrical and continuous. This can lead to changes – as when colliding billiard balls alter their respective trajectories or sugar dissolves in hot tea – or they can preserve the status quo – components of a sturdy bridge work together to maintain rigidity; two playing cards propped up support each other upright on a table top.

This would seem to be an advance over an influential conception of causation according to which causation is a relation among events that is

(1) *asymmetrical* (causes precede effects)
(2) *non-reflexive* (no event causes itself)
(3) *transitive* (if A causes B, and B causes C, then A causes C)
(4) whenever an A-type event occurs, it is accompanied by a B-type event (*constant conjunction*)

This list omits any sense that causes *bring about* or *necessitate* effects. Causes precede effects, but you can have one event's preceding another without the first's causing the second. Imagine an occasion on which clapping your hands is followed immediately by a flash of lightning. This, you assume, was mere coincidence: the flash of lightning accompanied, but was not caused by, your clapping. If you had any doubt about this, you might try clapping again. If, as is unlikely, repeated claps were invariably followed by flashes of lightning, you might come to think that somehow your clapping *did* somehow cause flashes of lightning.

You would have evidence of a *correlation* between two kinds of event: your clapping and lightning's flashing. As we learn early on, although the discovery of a correlation can be *evidence* of causation, something more is required. What might that be? Maybe the difference between a mere correlation and a genuine instance of causation is that causation, unlike correlation, is a *bringing about*.

That seems right, but what kind of evidence might you have that some occurrence did in fact bring about another? In the hand-clapping case, you might look for some kind of mechanism connecting your clapping and the occurrence of lightning flashes: an elaborate setup involving radio transmissions and water droplets making up clouds might work. Your clapping initiates a causal chain leading to a flash of lightning.

What of the links in the chain? Are these bringings about? If they are, how might you go about establishing that they are? You would be faced with further sequences – your clapping converted to radio waves via a microphone followed by a signal followed by a flash of lightning. (I leave it to you, the reader, to supply the details.) These really amount to more and finer-grained correlations. You might continue decomposing the mechanism all the way down to the particles and fields, discovering finer and finer-grained correlations. The question is, how might you move from these to genuine bringings about?

## 7.1 Aristotelianism

One possibility, mentioned in §5.3, is that correlation is *all there is* to causation. This idea is commonly associated with David Hume, and those who embrace it identify themselves as "Humeans." On the other side are the "Aristotelians," who regard causal sequences as genuine bringings about. (It is doubtful that Hume himself was a Humean, but that is beside the point: self-identified Humeans, at least, *are* Humeans. It is a little more likely that Aristotle was an Aristotelian.) Humeans profess never to observe bringings about, only correlations, and regard Aristotelians as mystery-mongers who introduce occult connections where there are none.

Aristotelians accept that evidence for bringings about consists in finding correlations. They argue that this is merely an *epistemological* matter, however, not something bearing directly on the metaphysics of causation. *Evidence* for causal connections is one thing, the *nature* of those connections, something else altogether. This is to take a *realist* position on causation. Causation is a real phenomenon "out there," something going beyond whatever counts as evidence for it.

But why think that? If your evidence consists only of correlations, how could you make the leap to bringings about? Aristotelians respond that, if you regard causation as the mutual manifestation of powers possessed by objects, you can explain *why* things behave as they do, thereby *explaining* the correlations and, ultimately, laws of nature. The supposition that the universe includes empowered objects, interacting in complex ways owing to their powerful natures, allows us to make sense of everyday experience and, significantly, the success of the sciences.

Humeans accuse Aristotelians of going beyond the evidence when they posit powers and depict causal sequences as mysterious bringings about. Aristotelians respond that if correlations were all there were, there would be a much greater mystery. What accounts for there being these correlations and not others? If we find that all observed *A*s are followed by *B*s, what would give us the right to expect the next *A* to be followed by a *B*? If you allow that objects' properties empower those objects, then similarly propertied *A*s would be similarly empowered, hence behave similarly in similar circumstances. This would provide a basis for laws of nature.

Laws are said to "govern" the behavior of objects. Newton's Third Law:

> When an object exerts a force on a second object, the second object simultaneously exerts a force equal in magnitude and opposite in direction on the first body.

*Why* does this law hold? And what could it mean to say that the law *governs* the behavior of objects?

Aristotelians have an answer. Every material body has a definite mass. By virtue of having the mass it has, an object has the power to exert an attractive force on other massive objects. This is not a one-sided affair:

objects exert forces in concert with other objects. This exercise of reciprocal powers is simultaneous and continuous. The Third Law captures all this in an eloquent way. Laws do not exert forces on objects, laws do not coerce or police objects. This is the job of objects' powers. Laws set out powers' job descriptions. Powers, not laws, govern.

An Aristotelian universe is a busy place teeming with activity. Power-imbued objects interact with one another to yield new configurations of objects that in turn yield further configurations. The universe evolves of necessity owing to its occupants' powerful natures.

Except sometimes. Some powers operate solo, or so physics tells us. When a radium atom decays, yielding an atom of radon and an α-particle, it does so on its own without provocation. There is no saying precisely when the atom will decay. (Isotopes of radium have "half-lives" ranging from a few seconds to 1,600 years. All we can say is that there is a 50 percent probability that the atom will decay over some period of time.)

The introduction of powers that operate without interacting with other powers is a refinement of the Aristotelian picture, not a departure from it. Radium atoms have definite half-lives, and when they decay, they do so in accord with their nature. Aristotelianism is a slam dunk! Why should anyone prefer a wimpy Humeanism to a muscular Aristotelianism? Humeans are content to skate on the surface. Aristotelians go behind the scenes to unveil the inner workings of the universe.

## 7.2 Humeanism

Why should anyone find Humeanism attractive? Thus far, I have focused on the Humean conception of causation. This conception is embedded within a larger picture and is best assessed in light of this larger picture.

The same is true of Aristotelianism. An Aristotelian, powers-based, account of causation is just one component of an inclusive map of the universe encompassing propertied, interacting substances. What is the Humean alternative?

What I have been calling Humeanism has a long history, but its current incarnation stems from the work of David Lewis (1941–2001) and ultimately from Lewis's teacher at Harvard, D. C. Williams (1899–1983). In a much-quoted passage, Lewis spells out what he calls "Humean supervenience":

> Humean supervenience is named in honor of the [great] denier of necessary connections. It is the doctrine that all there is to the world is a vast mosaic of local matters of particular fact, just one little thing after another. (But it is no part of the thesis that these local matters are mental.) We have geometry: a system of external relations of spatio-temporal distance between points. Maybe points of spacetime itself, maybe point-sized bits of matter or æther or fields, maybe both. And at these points we have local qualities: perfectly natural intrinsic properties which need nothing bigger than a point to be instantiated. For short: we have an arrangement of qualities. And that is all. There is no difference without difference in the arrangement of qualities. All else supervenes on that. (*Philosophical Papers*, vol. 2: ix–x)

Lewis invites you to think of the universe as consisting, not of interacting propertied substances, but a four-dimensional distribution of qualities. Every quality has a definite location in space and time. The qualities are not taken to be empowering. In a Humean universe, nothing interacts with anything else. You have a distribution of qualities, the "Humean mosaic." These no more interact or bring about changes than do the tiles on your kitchen floor. What we commonly think of as change over time is at bottom only qualitative variation in the temporal dimension (§2.1).

Imagine a tomato's ripening in the sun, gradually turning from green to red. The tomato is extended in time as well as space. In addition to its spatial parts, a top and a bottom, the tomato has temporal parts. One of these is green, another red. Intervening parts reflect the transition from green to red. Considered as a four-dimensional "worm," the tomato does not change. What we describe as the tomato's changing color is just its temporal parts exhibiting different colors – some are green, some are red, and others are shades somewhere between green and red.

This is what qualitative change amounts to in a Humean universe. What about motion, change in location? A billiard ball rolls across the billiard table and strikes another billiard ball. You can get a feel for how this works in a Humean universe by thinking of the motion of a televised billiard ball across a television screen. The televised ball's motion is really a sequence of pixels turning on then off. You do not have one spherical piece of matter occupying successive regions of the screen over time. You have only different patterns of illumination at different times.

What happens to causation in a Humean universe? Think of one billiard ball's striking another and causing both balls to alter their trajectories in familiar ways. Now, return to the televised ball. The ball moves across the screen, encounters a second ball, and both balls undergo changes in their respective trajectories. The motions are in reality nothing more than patterns of changes in the illumination of pixels. The balls on the screen do not initiate changes in one another; the changes are due to factors behind the scenes.

You can see how this works for objects "moving about" and "interacting" on television screens, but how would it work in reality? The television screen was meant to provide a limited analogy. Although patterns of pixel illumination on a television screen over time are not the result of earlier patterns, these patterns are brought about by offscreen occurrences. In the case of reality, however, there is no offscreen. A Humean universe just *is* patterns of qualities that make up the four-dimensional Humean mosaic. Each quality is a pixel, a small component in a massive array of pixels that constitutes the universe over time.

You experience the universe as a dynamic three-dimensional arrangement of interacting objects. You experience time passing. But, carrying through on the television screen analogy, you too are just a pattern of qualities. You are not a spectator on a changing scene; you are very much a part of the scene. Your experience of moving billiard balls amounts to one of your temporal parts experiencing temporal parts of the balls in one location, and one of your later temporal parts experiencing later temporal parts of the billiard balls in other locations. This is not far off McTaggart's *B* series discussed in chapter 2.

In that chapter I observed that spatial and temporal parts are not components of objects, but regions of space and time that include those objects. If complex wholes depend on their parts – the parts are "prior to" the whole – spatial and temporal parts depend on the wholes to which they belong – the wholes are prior to the parts.

This point is easily missed because we very often refer to material parts of objects by citing the region of space they occupy. Eastern Europe is not a spatial part of Europe, but the hills, valleys, border crossings, and rivers that occupy the eastern portion of the continent of Europe. I mention this because many philosophers mean by spatial and temporal parts portions of the occupants of regions of space and time.

When the universe is described as evolving over time, what you have is the universe exhibiting differences in the distribution of qualities at different temporal locations. Strictly speaking, the universe is not a something that evolves or undergoes changes. The universe simply is what it is: a four-dimensional arrangement of qualities. "As it was in the beginning, is now and ever shall be, world without end. Amen."

### Supervenience

Lewis says "We have an arrangement of qualities. And that is all. There is no difference without difference in the arrangement of qualities. All else supervenes on that." What is it to *supervene*? What is *supervenience*?

Philosophers use "supervenience" to mean many different things. For some, supervenience is a dependence relation among levels of properties. When the As supervene on the Bs, the As *depend on* but are *distinct from*, the Bs. This conception informs nonreductive physicalism and, in particular, the concept of multiple realizability (see §§3.4–3.7).

Although this conception of supervenience is consistent with what Lewis says, he more likely has in mind something closer to truthmaking (§3.7): when the As supervene on the Bs, truths couched in the A-vocabulary are made true by arrangements of Bs, even though A-vocabulary truths cannot be reduced to – that is translated or paraphrased in – the B-vocabulary.

## 7.3 Qualitied Somethings

Suppose Lewis is right, suppose the universe is a four-dimensional arrangement of qualities. The natural question to ask is, qualities of what? If you think of qualities as ways things are, modes, modifications, they must be qualities of *something*. That something cannot itself be a modification: a modification of a modification is just a facet of the modification itself. Think of a wrinkle in the tablecloth as a modification of the tablecloth. Now modify this wrinkle – by, for instance, putting an indentation down its center. The result is a new wrinkle, a new modification of the tablecloth. Just as wrinkles require something to be wrinkled, so qualities require somethings – substances – to be qualitied.

Lewis says "we have an arrangement of qualities. And that is all." What of space and time, or spacetime? If you have spatial and temporal locations, these seem to be locations *in* space and time. Are space and time themselves qualities overlapping all the others? If they are qualities, what is their qualitative nature?

Recall the discussion of fields in §6.5. Perhaps the qualities are qualities of fields or of a single unified field. This makes fields the bearers of qualities, the qualities being modifications of fields. Fields pervade spacetime, however, and this leaves the problem of locating spacetime (or space and time, a qualification I shall henceforth omit) in the Humean mosaic of qualities.

Another possibility is that the qualities are qualities *of* spacetime, spacetime taking on the substance role. Lewis himself suggests this without endorsing it explicitly. If Humean qualities are modes, a possibility that sits well with the Humean mosaic, then making them modifications – thickenings maybe, or energy concentrations – of spacetime would seem a promising option, although physics has the final call. To keep the discussion from being unnecessarily convoluted, I shall suppose that spacetime is the bearer of Lewis's qualities. If that is wrong, the metaphysical lessons in what follows would be largely unaffected.

## 7.4 Speculative Cosmology

Aristotelianism provides a satisfying Big Picture – what D. C. Williams calls a speculative cosmology – that nicely fits ordinary experience and much of what the sciences tell us. No imaginative leap is required to see the universe as populated by active, interacting objects that come and go, bring about changes in one another, and account for the evolving character of the universe. Humeanism, in contrast, offers a surprising and, in light of the availability of an attractive Aristotelian option, apparently unmotivated, cosmology.

Matters are not so simple, however. They never are in philosophy, and especially in metaphysics. You knew that was coming, right? Philosophers build castles in the air in the hope of distracting you from more pressing affairs. I hope to persuade you otherwise.

Aristotelianism works nicely under the assumption that the universe is made up of objects interacting in space over time. Indeed, causality seems tailored to such universes. If the universe turned out to be seamless in the manner depicted in §6.5, however, things would look very different. If objects were wrinkles in space-time, for instance, their "interactions" would amount to reconfigurations of spacetime, which themselves would amount to spacetime's being differently configured in different temporal regions.

Some philosophers object to the idea that time is spacelike, the idea that things are extended both in space and in time. For them you have persisting objects located in a three-dimensional space "moving through" time. Would this bring Aristotelianism back into play? Does Humeanism owe whatever plausibility it might be thought to have exclusively to the controversial assumption of a four-dimensional "block universe"? Absent that assumption, does Humeanism fall apart?

So long as the universe has a seamless character, Aristotelianism is threatened. Interacting objects – colliding billiard balls – would be ripples in space, or evolving energy concentrations in fields, or something of the sort. Although wave interference is a familiar physical phenomenon, the equations used to describe the changing face of the universe might be best understood as describing a whole, the universe, evolving over time.

## 7.5 Hylomorphism

Ironically, Aristotle himself embraced a seamless universe. Aristotle's universe comprised stuffs, not atoms.
The stuffs – fire, air, water, earth – could be mixed so
as to produce ordinary objects: natural objects (water
droplets, stones), artefacts (tables, goblets), and living
things (trees, rabbits). The character of each of these
was determined by its *form*. Objects assembled from the
elemental stuffs were said to be "compounds" of form
and matter.

This conception of the universe goes by the Greek
name, *hylomorphism* – from Greek *hylē* (matter) and
*morphē* (form). Hylomorphism has been historically
influential and, as philosopher Michael Rea observes,
"hylomorphism is on the rise in contemporary metaphysics" (Rea 2011: 342).

For Aristotle, the matter of an object such as a rabbit
was a variegated mixture of the four elemental stuffs.
What of its form? On some accounts, Aristotle's forms
were what I have been calling *essences*: the *what it is
to be* (this phrase, in fact, comes from Aristotle). So
conceived, essences are not entities. If Bunkin is a rabbit,
this is because Bunkin is what it is to be a rabbit, or as I
prefer, Bunkin has what it takes to be a rabbit.

On another reading of Aristotle, forms are active
agents causally responsible for anything's being what
it is. Bunkin's form would be responsible for bringing
it about that Bunkin is a rabbit, and not a cat or a
cabbage. Living things would seem to be examples of
entities, the nature of which ensures a measure of continuity over time. Bunkin grows and matures as he does
owing to internal mechanisms that oversee the process.

These competing accounts of Aristotle's forms reflect
two readings of "what makes it the case" that a thing is
what it is, what makes it the case that Bunkin is a rabbit,
for instance. As noted in §5.0, this could mean either

(1)  what *makes it true* that Bunkin is a rabbit
(2)  what *brought it about* that Bunkin is a rabbit

On the first interpretation, a form is not an entity but something closer to a definition. On the second interpretation, Bunkin's form is whatever in Bunkin is responsible for bringing it about that Bunkin is, and continues to be, a rabbit.

I am not competent to say which, if either, of these conceptions of form was Aristotle's. Scholars are divided, and contemporary advocates of hylomorphism are divided as well. Some think of form in the first way; others take form to be a "top-down," whole-to-part causal factor responsible for the unity of complex objects. Earlier, I noted the irony of calling a universe of interacting objects Aristotelian, given Aristotle's commitment to a seamless universe. The irony is lost on contemporary purveyors of hylomorphism, many of whom take for granted an atomistic universe and see hylomorphism as providing an answer to the special composition question (§§5.1–5.4).

## 7.6  A Humean Cosmology

A question remains. If the universe is granular, if the universe contains objects moving about and apparently interacting, is Humeanism foiled? If that were so, we would have to await the word of physicists, those who engage in non-speculative, empirical cosmology. The jury is still out, but, in my estimation, the preponderance of evidence favors a seamless cosmology.

I shall have more to say about this in the next chapter. First, however, it is worth considering the implications of a Humean, seamless cosmology for our everyday conception of things.

To all appearances, the lived-world, the universe as we conceive of it in going about our business, is one of interacting objects. These move about, persist over time despite undergoing sometimes dramatic changes, and affect and are affected by other objects. This impression informs scientific endeavors just as it does everyday life. Does this mean that if a Humean cosmology were apt, the universe as we encounter it would be an illusion?

Imagine a billiard ball's rolling across the table, colliding with another, with the result being a change in the balls' respective trajectories. Earlier I suggested that, given a Humean cosmology, this sequence would turn out to be something like its televised counterpart. When televised billiard balls move across the screen and collide, you have, not bits of the screen occupying successive regions and affecting one another's motion, but stationary pixels turning on and off in a certain pattern. Were the actual universe like this, it would seem that our experiences of the universe are illusory: the appearances disguise, rather than reveal, the nature of reality.

You might allow this as an abstract possibility, just as you might allow the possibility that the universe is wholly in your mind. But why should anyone take it seriously; why should anyone sincerely prefer a Humean cosmology to its Aristotelian counterpart? Under the circumstances, it seems preferable to stick with Aristotelianism (or, at any rate, a "granular" atomistic Aristotelianism) in the absence of compelling reasons to replace it with its Humean counterpart.

I hope you feel the pull of this way of thinking, but not because I am keen to convince you that it is correct. My hope, rather, is that you come to appreciate that these thoughts are metaphysical in character, further evidence of metaphysics' pervasiveness and inevitability. Once you see that, you are in a position to recognize alternatives.

Suppose the universe really were a four-dimensional array of qualities, and suppose change, motion, causal interaction, and the rest belong to the appearances: the deep story is something else altogether. This would not show that the appearances are illusory. It would show what the appearances are appearances *of*. This seems to be what Lewis has in mind in setting up the Humean mosaic. He says, in the passage quoted in §7.2: "we have an arrangement of qualities. And that is all. There is no difference without difference in the arrangement of qualities. All else supervenes on that."

One way to understand Lewis's cosmology is to see the Humean mosaic as providing truthmakers for all the truths, or, at any rate, all the truths about the universe. Thus, although it is true that the billiard ball moves, the truthmaker for this, surprisingly, turns out to be nothing that moves. Earlier I illustrated the point by comparing such a conception of motion to the motion of a televised billiard ball. The truthmaker for "the billiard ball moves across the screen" is nothing that itself occupies successive spatial locations. Motion – *motion* – across the screen just *is* stationary pixels turning on and off.

In the same way, you might think of the Humean mosaic, not as exposing our Aristotelian impressions as imposters, but as providing an account of what, at bottom, they are impressions of. Were a Humean cosmology correct, it would provide an account of what motion, change, and causation at bottom *are*. It is true that things change, move, and interact, but the truthmaker for all these truths might be a four-dimensional Humean mosaic.

Please do not imagine that I am urging you to buy Lewis's Humean picture. I myself am undecided. The important lesson is that, if you reject Humeanism in favor of Aristotelianism (or some other cosmology), you should do so for the right reasons. To reject it because it strikes you as patently at odds with the appearances is to misjudge it. Worse, it is to engage in sub-par metaphysics.

## Glossary

*Aristotelianism* and *Humeanism*. As used here, these are names for philosophical worldviews inspired by their namesakes, Aristotle and Hume, respectively. An Aristotelian universe includes empowered objects interacting and undergoing changes over time. In a Humean universe there are no powers, no interactions among "distinct existences," only evolving distributions of qualities.

*Cosmology.* A cosmology in this context is a metaphysical picture of the universe as a whole aimed at making sense of the universe as we encounter it in the laboratory and in everyday life. Aristotelianism and Humeanism advance competing cosmologies.

*Form.* For Aristotle, an essence, the what it is to be. The form or essence of a horse is what it is to be a horse.

*Humean mosaic.* For a Humean, the distribution of qualities over space and time that makes up a universe.

*Humean supervenience.* The view that the Humean mosaic provides truthmakers for all the truths that concern the universe and its contents.

*Hylomorphism.* A cosmology traceable to Aristotle according to which objects, or some objects, are compounds of form and matter. Philosophers differ in how they think of forms – for some, they are entities, for others they are what it is to be something of a particular kind. Hylomorphism is not a single doctrine, but a family of doctrines unified by the thought that whatever exists is made up of something (its matter) organized so as to be whatever it is (its form).

*Supervenience.* The term is used differently by different philosophers. Some regard it as a kind of dependence relation among families of properties. Thus, mental properties are sometimes said to supervene on physical properties, the idea being that your mental state is dependent on your physical state, but not identifiable with it. In contrast, others understand supervenience as truthmaking. If the mental supervenes on the physical, then mental truths have physical truthmakers. Despite their differences, both conceptions share a distaste for reductionism, the view that truths concerning the universe are all expressible in the vocabulary of physics.

## Further Readings

Although views I classify as Aristotelian are meant to cover a wide range of positions, the unifying factor is a conception of the universe as including powers that facilitate interactions among objects. "Humeans," in contrast, offer a picture of the universe bereft of powers. C. B. Martin would be an archetypal Aristotelian and David Lewis, his Humean counterpart. McTaggart and D. C. Williams would, on this classification, count as Humeans.

Lewis's formulation of "Humean Supervenience" appears in his *Philosophical Papers*, vol. 2 (New York: Oxford University Press, 1986: ix–x). I have substituted "great" for "greater," which occurs in the published version. Anthony Fisher informs me that Lewis made this correction in his own copy. You can appreciate the influence of Williams on his student, Lewis, by comparing the passage quoted on pages 2–3 of Williams's "Universals and Existents" (*Australasian Journal of Philosophy* 64 [1986]: 1–14).

On the Aristotelian side, Hugh Mellor's "In Defence of Dispositions" (*Philosophical Review* 83 [1974]: 157–81) was a pioneering work, as were Rom Harré and Edward Madden's *Causal Powers: A Theory of Natural Necessity* (Oxford: Basil Blackwell, 1975) and Nancy Cartwright's *Nature's Capacities and their Measurement* (Oxford: Oxford University Press, 1989). More recent exemplars include Brian Ellis, *Scientific Essentialism* (Cambridge: Cambridge University Press,

2001), Alexander Bird, *Nature's Metaphysics: Laws and Properties* (Oxford: Clarendon Press, 2007), and Anjan Chakravartty, *A Metaphysics for Scientific Realism* (Cambridge: Cambridge University Press, 2007).

Useful collections include Anna Marmodoro, *The Metaphysics of Powers* (London: Routledge, 2010) and Jon Jacobs, *Causal Powers* (Oxford: Oxford University Press, 2017). For a very different, counterfactual account of the inner workings of nature, see Marc Lange, *Natural Laws in Scientific Practice* (New York: Oxford University Press, 2000).

Aristotle's hylomorphism emerges in his *Physics* ii, 1, 193a 9–17 and *Metaphysics Z* and *H*, see William Charlton, *Aristotle: Physics Books I and II* (Oxford: Clarendon Press, 1970) and David Bostock, *Aristotle: Metaphysics Books Z and H* (Oxford: Clarendon Press, 1994). More recent discussions include Mark Johnston, "Hylomorphism" (*Journal of Philosophy* 103 [2006]: 652–98), Katherine Koslicki, *The Structure of Objects* (Oxford: Oxford University Press, 2008), Kit Fine, "Towards a Theory of Part" (*Journal of Philosophy* 107 [2010]: 559–89), Michael Rea, "Hylomorphism Reconditioned" (*Philosophical Perspectives* 25 [2011]: 341–58), and Simon Evnine, *Making Objects and Events: A Hylomorphic Theory of Artifacts, Actions, and Organisms* (Oxford: Oxford University Press, 2016). Fine's "Essence and Modality" is included in the suggested readings for chapter 6.

# 8

# Is this Chapter Really Necessary?

## 8.0 Necessitation

In setting out his Humean cosmology (§7.2), David Lewis speaks of Hume as "the [great] denier of necessary connections." Lewis had in mind Hume's attack on conceptions of causation according to which causes necessitate their effects. Necessitation figures in the idea that causes *bring about* – necessitate – their effects. To deny this is to deny that effects are present owing to causes.

Baldly stated this sounds preposterous. Surely everyday experience provides abundant evidence that causes are responsible for their effects. How could we account for the status of laws discovered by the sciences were this not so, were causal relations mere correlations among types of event?

Looked at in context, however, the Humean position as I am characterizing it proves less outlandish and more palatable. The context is provided by the Humean mosaic: the universe comprises a four-dimensional patchwork of qualities. The universe evolves over time, but nothing *in* the universe affects anything else. A Humean universe resembles a television screen. When an object moves across the screen, nothing on the screen moves. The object's "moving" amounts to a dynamic pattern of pixel illuminations. When televised billiard balls "collide" and their respective trajectories change, you have another pattern of pixels. The pixels do not themselves move or interact; the source of their antics is behind the scenes.

To be sure, this is only an analogy. In the situation the analogy is meant to illuminate, there is no behind-the-scenes. *All there is* to the universe is what is on the screen. Would this mean that in a Humean universe nothing moves or interacts with anything else, that motion and causation are illusory? Maybe not.

In §7.6 I suggested that, were physics to reveal that the universe is Humean, this would not be to abolish change, motion, or causation. It would be to reveal what these at bottom *are*. Truthmakers for "the ball moved" and "the billiard balls interacted so as to bring about changes in the velocity of both" would include nothing that moved, nothing that brought about anything.

A Humean universe contains no necessitation, only transitions from one state to another. This idea has struck many philosophers (and virtually all non-philosophers) as ridiculous on the face of it. I hope I have convinced you that, while it might be wrong, it is neither ridiculous nor out of keeping with everyday and scientific practice. I turn now to some of its implications and, in the process, introduce you to another important metaphysical topic.

## 8.1 Modality

The question whether causes "necessitate" their effects invokes the concept of necessity. Necessity is a *modal* concept, a concept belonging to a closely knit family of concepts that includes actuality, possibility, impossibility, and contingency. If something is possible, it is not impossible. If something is actual, it is also possible, hence not impossible. When something is necessary, it could not have been otherwise. Something is contingent when it is actual, but not necessary, when it could have been otherwise.

You exist, so your existence is possible. Is your existence contingent, could you have failed to exist? It would seem so. It is easy to call to mind how things could have been different so as to yield a universe in which you do not exist. Your parents might never have met, for instance, or Earth could have been vaporized after being struck by a colossal asteroid.

Of course, for your parents never to have met, a host of other things would have to have been different, and for each of these to have been different still more things would have had to be different. You might have heard of the Butterfly Effect: a small change in the initial conditions of complex – "chaotic" – systems can lead to momentous changes in the evolution of the system. A butterfly fluttering its wings in Brazil might play an indispensable role in the much later occurrence of a Hurricane in the Gulf of Mexico. Similarly, your failing to exist for whatever reason would bring with it unimaginably many changes in the landscape of the universe – past, present, and future.

Given that your existing is a consequence of a fragile network of causes and effects, it would seem to follow that not only is it possible that you could have failed to exist, but that your managing to exist is almost miraculous!

This line of reasoning, flattering as it might be for those of us who have succeeded in existing, rests on the assumption that the universe *could* have been different, which is just the original question all over again. Do you suppose that because you can imagine a different universe that different universe is possible? This equates possibility with imaginability or conceivability. Is that all there is to it, or is there something objectively real about possibility? Are there imaginable universes that are not in fact possible? For that matter, might it be the case that the universe we inhabit is the *only* universe possible? Were that so, the universe being as it is would not be contingent.

The universe might turn out to be contingent in a different way, however. It might not be contingent that the universe is as it is, but the universe itself might have failed to be. What if the universe issued from the Big Bang, and the Big Bang was a spontaneous fluctuation in the void, a cataclysmic occurrence resembling the spontaneous decay of a radium atom? Or suppose the universe was brought into being by an omniscient, omnipotent God freely choosing to do so.

Although the void might never have fluctuated and God might never have chosen to produce the universe, there is every reason to think that any occurrence of a fluctuation or God's choosing would have issued in the universe as it is. God chooses freely. God does not make mistakes, however, so it would seem that if God created any universe it would have been our universe.

The case of a spontaneous fluctuation in the void is no different. When an unstable element decays, its nature ensures that it does so spontaneously, its decaying is uncaused. But it is of the nature of the element that when it decays, it does so in a particular way. When a radium atom decays, the result is, not just *anything*, but an atom of radon and an α-particle. Even if the Big Bang were spontaneous, that need not mean that its outcome – our universe – could have been different than it is. Further, if time started with the Big Bang, it would make no sense to think that the Big Bang could have occurred earlier or later than it did.

None of this shows that the universe must be as it is, let alone that it could not have failed to be. What it does show is that, if you think that what is or is not possible, what is or is not contingent, is an objective matter, the contingency of the universe, or anything else, would need to be established. How? One source of contingency might be the kind of spontaneity just discussed, a topic to which I shall return in due course.

## 8.2 Alternative Universes

Philosophically sophisticated readers might wonder why I have neglected a popular device for explicating modality: David Lewis's possible worlds, or, as I prefer, alternative universes. According to Lewis, something is possible if it occurs at some alternative universe, impossible if it occurs at none. Something is absolutely necessary if it occurs at every alternative universe. The necessity of water's being $H_2O$ would be due to its being true that water is $H_2O$ at every universe containing water.

Your existence is contingent – you could have failed to exist – if there are alternate universes in which you are absent. Alternative universes are commonly invoked by philosophers to explicate the conditions under which contrary-to-fact – counterfactual – assertions are true. It is true that had you dropped this fragile teacup it would have shattered if, in universes most similar to ours and in which a counterpart of you drops a counterpart of this cup, it shatters.

A word about counterparts is in order. You and the cup are in this universe, and no other. Other universes contain counterpart yous, counterpart cups. These are more or less perfect duplicates of you and the cup. In this universe, the actual universe, you do not drop the cup and the cup does not shatter. But there are other, very similar universes in which someone very similar to you drops a very similar cup, and that cup shatters.

But wait! The discussion began by asking how genuine, objective possibilities might be established. It would seem that explicating possibilities by appealing to alternative universes, Lewis's possible worlds, simply begs the question, assuming the very point at issue. How could we know whether any of those other universes really *are* possible? And, anyway, why should anything going on in a phony alternative universe have any bearing on what goes on here and now?

Lewis's universes are not meant to be limpid fictions, not merely figures of speech or metaphors. Recall the discussion (in §7.2) of Lewis's Humean cosmology, the doctrine that the universe comprises a four-dimensional array of qualities, the Humean mosaic. If you take this cosmology seriously, there is no place for talk about possibilities to take hold. There is the universe as it is, the four-dimensional Humean mosaic of qualities. If this is meant to serve as the ground of *all* the truths concerning what there is, then the most we can say of anything is that it is what it is. In fact, because there is nothing to support the assertion that anything could have been different, the whole setup exudes, if anything, an air of necessity!

Still, we rely on talk of possibilities, necessities, bringings about, and contrary-to-the-fact facts to good effect. How could Lewis hope to account for the utility of modal concepts and their application to the universe?

Aristotelians have an answer. The universe is made up of a massively interactive collection of empowered objects. Once you have the measure of these powers, you can say what an object could or could not do in concert with other objects. You can say with confidence that a fragile teacup would shatter were it dropped, because we have a grasp of powers inherent in the teacup and the hard surface beneath it.

Humeans reject talk of powers: nothing *in* the universe brings about anything else, nothing *in* the universe is responsible for anything else's being as it is. When it comes to modality, a Humean's only resource is similarity. To say that something is possible is to say that it is similar to something actual. To say that the teacup would have shattered had you dropped it is to say that situations in which comparable teacups are dropped and shatter are more similar to actual situations than those in which similar cups are dropped on similar surfaces and fail to shatter.

As observed in §7.0, when you look at what would constitute evidence in such cases, it does indeed seem to be the case that we appeal to similarities in the form of correlations, what Hume called "constant conjunction."

## 8.3  Logical Possibility

You might wonder where this leaves the objectivity of judgments about what is or is not possible, judgments about what must, might, or might not have occurred. Aristotelians can appeal to powers, but similarities might be thought to reside in the eye of the beholder. Any two complex situations might be similar in *some respects*, dissimilar in others. A red ball is similar to a red cube with respect to its color, but not with respect to its shape. When it comes to complex situations, similarity is not all or nothing.

Start with our universe, the Humean mosaic in which you and I reside. Consider all the *logically possible* – consistently statable – rearrangements of qualities in the Humean mosaic. These massively outstrip our imaginations, but they are what they are quite independently of our imaginative powers. Next, consider all these logically possible variations in which elements are subtracted, all the way down to universes with a single instantaneous quality. Finally, consider universes that include "alien" qualities not found in the actual universe, and, again, all the variations on these. Each of these occupies a unique location in the vast space of logical possibility; each encompasses an alternative universe.

We commonly distinguish logical possibility from real

or natural possibility. Although it is logically possible that a lump of coal could survive intact in a fiery furnace, we do not think of this as a serious possibility. Something is logically possible if it can be described without contradiction. The survival of the lump of coal is logically possible, but it is *not* logically possible that $7 + 5 \neq 12$. Given what these symbols mean, the expression could not be true under any circumstances.

Alternative universes can be objectively similar to our universe in some respects, but not in others. Two teacups could be similar in respect to their colors, but dissimilar in respect to their makeup: one is ceramic, the other plastic. When you ask whether this cup would have broken if you had dropped it, the cups' respective colors are not relevant, but their makeup would be. This, however, is not because differences in makeup mean differences in powers, but because objects made of ceramic generally shatter when dropped on hard surfaces, and those made of plastic do not.

Similarity is not a transitive relation. $A$ can be similar to $B$, $B$ to $C$, and $C$ to $D$, while $A$ and $D$ are not similar. This is so even when you consider *respects* in which objects are similar. The color of $A$ might be similar to that of $B$, $B$'s to that of $C$, and $C$'s to that of $D$, without $A$'s color being similar to $D$'s. The space of logical possibilities grades off into spaces that resemble our universe in no respect whatever, universes altogether out of reach of our imaginations or conceptual resources.

Notice that the space of logical possibilities is wholly filled; *every* logical possibility is included. Among other things, this affords a straightforward answer to the age-old question, why is there something rather than nothing? Nothing would be an unoccupied region of the logical spaces and an unoccupied region is not a region: nothing is not an option!

One more feature of this way of thinking about possibility and necessity is worth remarking on. Strictly speaking, nothing could have been other than it is. Could you have had a different number of hairs on your head? Certainly there is a logically possible counterpart of you with a different number of hairs, but the counterpart is not you. The only you is you just as you are. Anyone with a different number of hairs is not you. Nor could you have failed to exist. The space of logical possibilities includes every possibility, every alternative universe. You, precisely as you are, contribute in a modest way to the region of the space of possibilities you happen to occupy.

Lewis argues that logical possibilities are all the possibilities we need. Other senses of possibility – possibilities consistent with laws of nature, for instance, possibilities we consider real (and not *merely* logical) can, he holds, be extracted from these. The impossibility in our universe of a lump of coal's surviving unscathed in a furnace is explained by the fact that universes in which such lumps survive under comparable circumstances are dissimilar to ours in significant ways. In those universes the laws of nature might be different, for instance, or coal might be differently constituted.

## 8.4 Painless Modal Realism

Doubtless you are growing impatient with all this space-of-logical-possibilities talk. These logical spaces are, after all, merely abstract logical constructions, not concrete actualities. Lewis disagrees, endorsing "modal realism," according to which alternative universes are as real as the one in which we happen to reside: "I advocate a thesis of a plurality of worlds, or *modal realism*, which holds that our world is but one among many" (*On the Plurality of Worlds*: 2, original emphasis).

> When I profess realism about possible worlds, I mean to be taken literally. Possible worlds are what they are, and not some other thing. If asked what sort of thing they are,

I cannot give the kind of reply my questioner probably expects: that is, a proposal to reduce possible worlds to something else.

I can only ask him to admit that he knows what sort of thing our actual world is, and then explain that possible worlds are more things of that sort, differing not in kind but only in what goes on at them. (*Counterfactuals*: 85)

You likely side with many philosophers and reject out of hand the idea that alternative universes, discrete regions of a densely populated space of logical possibilities, are as real as our universe. Alternative universes are not concrete entities. They are merely logical constructs belonging to the realm of *abstracta*.

The time has come for me to explain my preference for talk of "alternative universes" to the more common "possible worlds." It is important to Lewis's position that all the worlds are on a par. Our world, our universe, is just one among many. Describing our universe as *actual* and the others as *possible* could suggest to impressionable minds that our universe has special standing among the universes: ours is actual, the others *merely* possible.

But why does Lewis regard all those other universes as on a par with ours? Why not just regard them as logical constructs? One way to make sense of modal realism is to begin by accepting that the logical possibilities are what they are quite objectively. Some amount to rearrangements of qualities in our universe. Some include fewer constituents, some more. Because the whole space of logical possibilities outruns human intellectual and imaginative capacities, it is what it is independently of us.

This might be all you need to side with Lewis. The space of logical possibilities is what does the work, and that is what it is quite objectively. And, come to think of it, all those other universes *do* seem to be on a par with ours: painless modal realism!

## 8.5  A Spinozistic Cosmology

The emerging picture, surprisingly, is one entirely lacking in contingency: everything is what it is of necessity. Why think that? Surely, Lewis, along with everyone else who has imbibed the wine of possible worlds, alternative universes, opens the door to endless possibilities. There are endless alternative universes!

Some might be happy to leave it at that, but I doubt that this "what, me worry?" attitude is warranted. Once you understand the unrelenting necessity of the space of logical possibilities and its occupants, Lewis's Humean universe begins to resemble the universe of a philosopher you might have thought inimical to Lewis: Baruch (in Latin, Benedictus) Spinoza (1632–1677). This is especially so when you consider the Humean mosaic.

Spinoza's cosmology resembles the cosmology of McTaggart, discussed in chapter 2. The universe, all there is, is a single simple substance analogous to spacetime. Call this the One. (Spinoza would have known nothing of spacetime, a relatively recent notion, but I believe it comes closest to capturing in contemporary terms what Spinoza had in mind.) Spinoza identified the One with God, but also with nature, describing it as *Deus, sive Natura*: God, or Nature. This identification is interesting, but it will not play a major role in what follows.

The One could be completely described in infinitely many ways, although finite minds were only cognizant of two of these: the mental and the material. Science attempts to construct a complete account of the One framed in terms of material bodies, which were, for Spinoza as for Descartes, modes of extension, ways of being extended, modifications of the One in so far as the One is extended.

What of the mental? Think of the mental as a kind of

field that permeates space. Here and there in the field, you find wrinkles or concentrations of psychic energy. These coincide with conscious minds.

As in the case of both the Humean mosaic and a "seamless" universe, what we commonly regard as objects turn out to be modes, modifications of the One. The One evolves over time as it does of necessity. The resulting cosmology closely resembles Lewis's Humean cosmology as I have characterized it. The universe amounts to a single propertied substance, the One, the nature of which ensures that it is what it is, was, and will be of necessity.

At first glance, this might seem dramatically different from Lewis's Humeanism. Every ingredient in the Humean mosaic is "loose and separate," nothing affects or influences anything else, and this would seem to be at odds with Spinoza's universal necessitarianism.

Spinoza's objects are modes, modifications of the One. As I read Lewis, the qualities that make up the Humean mosaic are most naturally understood as modes. In both cases, objects' antics are not a matter of modes interacting with one another, but expressions of the whole. Considered side by side, modes are loose and separate. The explanation for the evolution of the mosaic resides, not in the modes, but in the nature of what they modify: for Spinoza, the One, and for Lewis, perhaps spacetime.

This excursion into speculative cosmology is meant to illustrate a theme pervading this book, namely that metaphysics is a package deal. I have marched you through the territory in a linear fashion (how else could you march?) but metaphysical theses are not evaluable on their own, in isolation from one another. The question is always, how do they hang together – and with whatever we think we know about the universe as revealed by everyday experience and the sciences?

Spinoza and Lewis's Hume would appear to be at opposite ends of the spectrum. Taken altogether, however, their cosmologies converge in surprising fashion. At least that is how it seems to me. If I am wrong, not much is lost. I will have accomplished my purpose if I have managed to get you to think about the universe and our place in it in a way that might not have occurred to you before you picked up this book.

## Glossary

*Logical possibility.* Something is logically possible if it can be consistently described, described without contradiction. "Pigs fly" expresses a logical possibility, but "$12 - 7 = 6$" does not. We commonly distinguish *mere* logical possibilities (pigs fly) from real (or genuine) possibilities.

*Modality.* Possibility, actuality, and necessity, together with their contraries, impossibility, nonactuality (nonexistence), and contingency anchor the family of modal concepts. Something can be possible, but not actual, but if something is actual, it must also be possible. If something is necessary, it is both actual and possible.

*Possible world.* An alternative universe resembling the (actual) universe to a greater or lesser extent – and, in some cases, not at all. These are invoked in some accounts of modal truths: something is said to be possible if it occurs at some possible world, for instance, actual if it occurs here at our world.

## Further Readings

Modality – actuality, possibility, necessity, and their contraries – is an immense and difficult topic. The chapter's focus is on my own preferred way of making sense of David Lewis's appeal to "possible worlds" to explicate possibility, necessity, contingency, and various other modal concepts as is set out in his *On the*

*Plurality of Worlds* (Oxford: Basil Blackwell, 1986) and *Counterfactuals* (Cambridge, MA: Harvard University Press, 1973). I should warn you that, with the possible exception of members of my immediate family, few approve of my way of spelling out Lewis's modal realism.

Discussions of the nature of modality are often technical. Saul Kripke's *Naming and Necessity* (mentioned in the suggested readings for chapter 6) is an important milestone. Kripke's approach is reminiscent of Locke's discussion of "real essences" that was addressed in chapter 6. Kit Fine, in "Essence and Modality," and E. J. Lowe, in "Metaphysics as the Science of Essence" (both cited in the suggested readings for chapter 6) take a somewhat different approach. Two collections, one edited by Tamar Gendler and John Hawthorne, *Conceivability and Possibility* (Oxford: Clarendon Press, 2002), and a second, edited by Andy Egan and Brian Weatherson, *Epistemic Modality* (Oxford: Oxford University Press, 2011) include papers reflecting a wide range of positions. Many of these would prove challenging to readers not already familiar with the territory.

In addressing Lewis's modal realism, I have omitted discussion of popular competitors: "fictionalism" (the alternative universes are useful fictions) and its cousin, "ersatz modal realism." I have done so for two reasons. First, the topic is technical and thereby falls outside the purview of a book aimed at the uninitiated. Second, I am convinced that possibility, necessity, and the like are baked into the nature of reality, a position I associate with the kind of "ontologically serious" metaphysics I have been doing my best to exemplify in these pages. This is not meant as an oblique criticism of positions I have not discussed; it is only to clarify my aims and distinguish them from the aims of others.

Finally, Yitzhak Melamed's *Spinoza's Metaphysics: Substance and Thought* (Oxford: Oxford University Press, 2013) affords an excellent introduction to

Spinoza's metaphysics. Michael Della Rocca's *Spinoza* (London: Routledge, 2008) is more wide ranging, but includes lucid discussions of themes touched on in this chapter.

# 9

# Conscious Minds

## 9.0 Body and Mind

You have a body, a complex organism crammed with complex components, and you have a mind. You know, well enough, what your body is and where it is – wherever you are! Others, physicians and scientists, know, or at any rate could come to know, much more about your body. What of your mind? You are at least as aware of your mind as you are of your body. But what do you really know about your mind, and what do the experts say?

Psychologists and psychiatrists study the mind, and do indeed have much to tell us. Neuroscientists investigate the brain and the nervous system. When they do, are they too studying the mind? When a neurosurgeon probes the brain of a patient, is the neurosurgeon probing the patient's mind? No one doubts that minds and brains are intimately related. Changes in the brain can have important effects on the mind. Why not say that the brain – or the brain plus the nervous system, a qualification I shall henceforth omit – *is* the mind?

At least two barriers stand in the way of identifying minds with brains. First, many philosophers, psychologists, and cognitive scientists insist that it is a mistake to regard minds as *things*. Brains, they contend, amount to organic computing machines. Your mind is a program running on neural hardware, and a program is not a piece of hardware.

A second barrier to the identification of minds with brains centers on consciousness. Conscious experiences have a distinctive gauzy "phenomenal" character. When you see a red billiard ball on a green felt table, you can describe how the ball and its surroundings *look* to you, how they *appear*. The looks of things, their appearances, belong, it would seem, not to the things, but to your experiences. When you close your eyes, your experience ceases, but the ball persists unaffected. Your experience of the ball is one thing, the ball another.

The difficulty of understanding how conscious experiences are related to brains persists even if you are happy to accept that minds are programs. You can see how many cognitive activities might be programmable. You can program a computer to check your spelling, prove a theorem, or even to write a poem. But it is much harder to see how conscious experiences could be programmed into your brain. Consciousness would seem more closely connected to your neural hardware than to your software. Consciousness can be a *vehicle* for thoughts, but there is more to being conscious than merely computing.

## 9.1 Mental Phenomena

The special character of conscious experiences has puzzled many. Some, proponents of *dualism*, hold that conscious experiences are nonmaterial. This option is fraught with difficulties of the kind mentioned in §3.1, however. The billiard ball, in concert with ambient light radiation, affects complex organs that make up your visual system, culminating in your visually experiencing the ball. Your visual experience guides you as you walk across the room to pick up the ball. If, however, your experience is mental and your body is made up of matter, how could the one affect or be affected by the other? How could a material thing impress itself on something nonmaterial? And how could a nonmaterial thing get a grip on something material?

A proponent of dualism might reply that causal interaction between mental things and things made up of matter, material things, is special, not at all like ordinary physical causation. What would evidence for mental–material interaction look like? Perhaps if we discovered inexplicable causal gaps in the operation of brains, these would require filling by nonmaterial causes. No such gaps have been discovered, however. The operation of material bodies seems completely explicable without introducing additional nonmaterial causal factors.

Difficulties attending mental–material causal interaction have led some dualists to embrace *epiphenomenalism*: mental states accompany, but do not affect, material states. Conscious experiences are analogous to the squeak made by a machine that accompanies, but plays no role in the machine's operation.

Although epiphenomenalism preserves the insights afforded by dualism while avoiding mysteries inherent in mental–material interaction, many find the thought that our mental states play no role in our actions deeply implausible. Surely your conscious decision to walk across the room had a part in your walking across the room.

Even if you are comfortable with the thought that conscious states are epiphenomenal, however, a difficulty remains. Neuroscientists sometimes refer to the brain as the "substrate" of consciousness. This suggests that consciousness is a product of neurological occurrences.

But how could a brain, a material system, produce or give rise to anything nonmaterial?

Scientists investigating the brain and philosophers often speak of mental–material *correlations*: mental states are correlated with brain states. Presumably, if the As are correlated with the Bs, the As and Bs are distinct. The neural correlates can be identified and measured, but what of the mental correlates? How are these investigated and measured?

In the sciences, correlations are commonly taken as evidence for causal relations. If conscious states were caused by material states, then it would be no wonder that the two are correlated. But the question remains: how could nonmaterial conscious states be produced by material occurrences? As Colin McGinn puts it, "how can Technicolor phenomenology arise from soggy grey matter?" ("Phenomenology" refers to the qualitative character, the *feel*, of your conscious experiences.)

Is all this just philosophical mystery-mongering? Perhaps. Nevertheless, the problem, what David Chalmers calls the Hard Problem, has occupied the attention of physicists and neuroscientists no less than philosophers. Chalmers is the force behind an annual conference that, prior to 2016, was called "Toward a Science of Consciousness." This is an impressive international affair that brings together philosophers and scientists of all stripes. After 2016, the conference was rebranded "The Science of Consciousness" conference, suggesting that progress has been made. Has it?

## 9.2 Origins of the Hard Problem

How did we get to this point? Historians of philosophy have observed that the Hard Problem is not one that would have gripped ancient philosophers nor, for that matter, medieval philosophers. Its origin appears to be in the seventeenth century at the dawn of the scientific revolution. As scientists began looking closely at the material universe, they noticed that there are important differences between the properties of material objects and our experiences of those objects.

You experience a billiard ball as red and warm to the touch. If you struck the ball with a billiard cue, the result would be a clicking noise. When you examine the ball closely, however, you learn that it is made up of color-less particles. The ball's warmth stems from the motions of some of these particles, and the sound it makes is a spherical pattern of vibrations in the air. What explains the disparity between the ball as you experience it, and the ball as it is in itself?

One explanation appealed to a distinction between *primary* and *secondary qualities*. Primary qualities – the billiard ball's shape, size, mass, for instance – are pre-sent in the ball. Secondary qualities, in contrast – the ball's perceived color, the sound you hear when the ball is struck, the warmth you feel when you hold the ball in your hand – are not in the ball but in you the observer. Secondary qualities are brought about in observers by complexes of primary qualities. If the colorless particles making up the ball's surface are arranged in one way, the result is a ball that looks red (at least to a normal human observer). Arrange the same particles differently and the result is a ball that looks green.

You might, then, distinguish the ball's redness (in actuality an arrangement of colorless particles) from *perceived redness* or *phenomenal redness*, which is in the observer. The same would hold for sounds, smells, tastes, and feelings of heat and cold. Thus conceived, seen colors, heard sounds, smelled smells, tasted tastes are not qualities of anything "out there." They are qual-ities of our conscious experiences we "project" onto objects. Philosophers call these qualities *qualia*.

Now the Hard Problem asserts itself. Scientists inves-tigating the material universe can focus on objects' primary qualities, relegating the rest to the minds of observers. This is a convenient strategy if your interest is solely in explaining material goings-on. Eventually, however, someone is bound to wonder about the status of conscious experiences. If you begin by bifurcating the universe into a material realm and a nonmaterial mental realm, the natural question is, how are these related? How might *qualia* make peace with the material universe?

*Materialism* offers one answer: there is no nonmaterial realm of *qualia*. The material realm is all there is. Maybe the mind just *is* the brain, and conscious processes just *are* brain processes.

For many, materialism does not solve, but simply ignores, the Hard Problem. If a billiard ball's perceived redness is not in the billiard ball, how could it be in the brain, which is, after all, no less a material thing than the ball. If you, working with a neuroscientist, were to scan my brain while I am looking at a red billiard ball, would you expect to see my red experience, an instance of phenomenal red?

What if you did, what if you observed colorful pictures in my brain, displayed perhaps on a tiny television screen? Implausible, perhaps, but even if you did, my having colorful experiences would remain mysterious. If perceiving a red ball were a matter of having a colorful internal image of the ball, this image would itself require an internal observer, a "homunculus," and the original difficulty is repeated. When the homunculus perceives the image, does the homunculus have an internal image? If so, does the homunculus have its own homunculus observing the first homunculus's image? And does that second homunculus have its own homunculus observing *its* internal image? The explanatory buck is passed with the consequence that nothing is explained. The upshot: any explanation of visual imagery that itself appeals to imagery explains nothing.

## 9.3 Emergence

In response to the Hard Problem, some philosophers and scientists have argued that mental phenomena "emerge" from nonmental, material phenomena provided that material is organized in the right way. *Qualia*, mental qualities, are emergent in the sense that they are qualities of complex systems, qualities lacked by the parts.

The idea that complexes could themselves have properties was discussed in chapters 4 and 5. After a certain amount of toing-and-froing, I offered reasons to doubt that complexes had properties. It is true that a cricket ball is red and spherical, despite being made of parts that are neither red nor spherical. The truthmaker for this is not a new property, sphericality, possessed by the ball, but simply the collection organized as it is. The collection has a distinctive organization, but no new properties.

Proponents of emergence agree – up to a point. They accept that most of what we informally regard as properties of complex systems are merely "resultant" – they are what you get when you arrange things in the right way; they are not properties of wholes in addition to the parts and their properties arranged as they are. A billiard ball's mass, for instance, is just the sum of the masses of its constituent particles.

Emergentists argue that, in some cases, when you put things together in the right way, a new whole with new properties arises. The whole and its properties are not merely resultant, but emergent. I would provide a simple uncontroversial example of emergence if I could, but I am not aware of any simple uncontroversial examples.

One reason for this is that there is considerable controversy concerning what emergence *is*. Some say that something is emergent if truths about it cannot be deduced from truths concerning their parts and their arrangement. Others characterize emergent phenomena as wholes governed by laws that cannot be deduced from laws governing their parts. To understand why a complex mechanical device does what it does you need only understand the laws governing the operations of its parts. An emergent entity would be one the behavior of which could be explained only by introducing new laws not extractable from laws governing its parts.

On either account, emergence would be nothing special metaphysically. Truths about *most* complex wholes cannot be deduced from truths about their parts. Emergence, so conceived, is called *weak emergence*. If this is what emergence amounted to, it would be both unremarkable and unsuitable as a potential solution to the Hard Problem. Pointing out that you could not deduce truths about my conscious experiences from truths about my neurophysiology merely restates the problem. If emergence is to be of use in solving the Hard Problem, it must be something more than weak emergence.

*Strong emergence* to the rescue! Strong emergence is meant to be more metaphysically robust than weak emergence. Although there is little consensus on what strong emergence would be, it is often explicated by reference to "top down" or "downward" causation. Downward causation occurs when wholes exert "configurational forces" over their parts. Are there examples? Here is Nobel laureate Roger Sperry (1913–1994):

> Subjective mental phenomena are conceived to influence and govern the flow of nerve impulse traffic by virtue of their encompassing emergent properties. Individual nerve impulses and other excitatory components of a cerebral activity pattern are simply carried along or shunted this way or that by the prevailing overall dynamics of the whole active process (in principle – just as drops of water are carried along by a local eddy in a stream or the way the molecules or atoms of a wheel are carried along when it rolls down the hill, regardless of whether the individual molecules and atoms happen to like it or not). ("A Modified Concept of Consciousness": 534)

Sperry's examples are unhelpful. The eddy does not act on the drops of water making it up; the eddy just *is* these drops moving in these ways. The wheel just *is* the particles that make it up; there is no question of the *wheel*'s exerting a force over those particles thereby altering their trajectories.

As matters stand, characterizing conscious phenomena as emergent and capable of exerting downward, top-down causal influence on parts of the complex system from which they emerge, is to say no more than somehow, when you put neurons together in the right way, poof! consciousness arises – and perhaps exerts a downward, configurational force on individual neurons. We are no closer to a solution to the Hard Problem.

Some philosophers (and many more nonphilosophers) have at this point thrown up their hands and embraced epiphenomenalism as the lesser of evils. By accepting *qualia*, qualitatively imbued conscious experiences, epiphenomenalism saves the appearances. Because conscious experiences are impotent biproducts of material processes, they can be safely ignored. Epiphenomena cannot intrude on the material universe, so they call for no scientific explanation. Still, we are left wondering how anything nonmental could somehow give rise to something mental.

## 9.4 Panpsychism

Recently, some philosophers have turned to a doctrine long regarded as discredited: *panpsychism*. Panpsychists hold that conscious qualities pervade the universe. The materialist mistake is to strip them away from matter. Galen Strawson, an exponent of panpsychism, calls this "real materialism": *materialism* because it accepts the hegemony of matter, *real* because it does not try to sweep conscious qualities under the rug or render them epiphenomenal.

Panpsychists observe that the physical sciences are bent on describing objects' powers, and so ignore their intrinsic qualitative nature. The fact that physics says nothing about the intrinsic qualitative nature of electrons and protons, however, does not license the conclusion that they have no intrinsic qualitative nature. They must! You and your brain are made up of the same kinds of particle that make up everything else. You are conscious, your experiences are qualitatively saturated. The best explanation for this is that the particles themselves have experiential qualities. We explain the mass of ordinary material bodies by supposing that the particles making them up have mass. In the same way, we could explain how you and I are conscious by supposing that the particles that make us up have, in addition to mass, qualitative experiential natures.

Throughout this discussion I have been supposing that the universe is granular, supposing that you and I, along with everything else, are interactive arrangements of particles. I have done so because the topics I have been addressing are almost always considered in these terms. You might have suspected that the presumption of a universe of particles is at least partly to blame for the Hard Problem. If the universe turned out to be seamless, McTaggart's universe, for instance, or Spinoza's, the difficulties might evaporate.

Indeed Spinoza, the hero of §8.5, affords an interesting example of a kind of seamless panpsychism. In discussing Spinoza's cosmology, I noted that, for Spinoza, consciousness is an attribute pervading the universe, something like a field suffusing spacetime. Were that so, conscious minds might be local concentrations of psychic energy in the consciousness field coinciding with material densities that make up the bodies or brains of conscious creatures.

This might in fact be the most plausible form of panpsychism. At present there is no evidence for the existence of such a field, however, and it is hard to imagine what evidence for it would look like.

## 9.5  Back to Basics

We have landed between a rock and the Hard Problem. Is there any way out that does not involve epiphenomenalism, emergence, or panpsychism?

Attempts to solve the Hard Problem differ in the details, but most share a common core of metaphysical assumptions. These constrain the discussion in ways that all but guarantee failure. As is so often the case in philosophy, problems are created by innocent-seeming presuppositions that are anything but. What happens when you look more closely at the metaphysical background?

If your aim is to understand minds and their properties, you need first to understand properties. Although I doubt that it affects the matter at hand, suppose properties are not universals but tropes, or better, modes (§§4.2 and 4.5). Properties are particular, nontransferable qualitative modifications of substances.

To keep the discussion from becoming impossibly abstract, suppose, as well, that the universe is a universe of particles. Again, I do not think this assumption biases the discussion, and, in any case, it is widely shared by philosophers and nonphilosophers who address the Hard Problem.

Properties, then, are qualities, qualitative modifications of substances that empower those substances in various ways. Scientists focus on the empowering nature of qualities, but, as Strawson observes, it would be a mistake to interpret scientists' silence on properties' qualitative natures as a denial that properties are qualitative as well as empowering. This is so for all properties, including properties of the unobservable particles. The fact that we never *observe* the qualities of unobservable particles is wholly unremarkable. We observe only the effects their presence has on instruments designed to detect them.

One obstacle to progress on the Hard Problem is a tacit assumption that material bodies themselves lack qualities. If qualities come to be only with the advent of conscious experiences, they must be add-ons (epiphenomenalism, emergence), or they, the conscious qualities, must already be present in the particles (panpsychism). If you reject this assumption and grant that qualitativity is everywhere, not solely in conscious experiences, you have disarmed one component of the Hard Problem.

Accepting that qualities are spread on the universe is not to embrace panpsychism. The idea, rather, is that the fact that you can get conscious qualities by putting together things with nonconscious qualities, is no more surprising than the fact that you can get something spherical by putting together things that are not spherical.

The possibility that minds might be brains, mental states and processes might be brain states and processes was mentioned in §9.2 and set aside as unworkable. One apparently insurmountable difficulty for the identification of minds with brains stems from the conviction that qualities of conscious experiences are nothing like anything you would expect to find in the brain.

Suppose that I am undergoing a vivid conscious experience of a red billiard ball. Were my experience a brain process, it could, in principle, be observed by a suitably equipped observer. Imagine that you are such an observer. You have come into possession of a cerebroscope, an instrument that allows you to observe minute occurrences in my brain. To complete the picture, suppose that my qualitatively rich experience *is* a particular occurrence in my brain, and you are observing that very occurrence.

At this point the Hard Problem reasserts itself. My experience of the red ball is qualitatively rich, but the neurological process you are observing reveals only "soggy gray matter," and that is nothing at all like my experience. How, then, could anyone seriously think that it *is* my experience?

## 9.6  Mary Learns Something New

Frank Jackson drives this point home in a famous thought experiment. Imagine Mary, a "brilliant scientist"

> who is, for whatever reason, forced to investigate the world from a black and white room *via* a black and white television monitor. She specialises in the neurophysiology of vision and acquires, let us suppose, all the physical information there is to obtain about what goes on when we see ripe tomatoes, or the sky, and use terms like "red," "blue," and so on. ("Epiphenomenal Qualia": 130)

One day Mary is released from her black and white room. Jackson asks, "will she learn anything?" The answer is clear. Yes! She will learn *what it is like* to have colored experiences; she will learn *what it is like* to experience red. Her exhaustive knowledge of the neurophysiology of color vision would not enable her to know (or even guess) what it is like to experience colors. In her black and white environment, Mary, despite knowing all there is about the material basis of color vision, is ignorant of this fact. Jackson concludes that the fact Mary comes to know something new – what it is like to experience colors – must concern something nonmaterial. Its undetectability means that it must be epiphenomenal.

We are back with the Hard Problem.

## 9.7  What Is it Like to Experience an Experience?

Before throwing in the towel, return to the case of your observing my brain. I am undergoing a visual experience of a red billiard ball. You in contrast, are, thanks to the cerebroscope, undergoing a visual experience, not of the ball, but of an occurrence in my brain, which, we are supposing, *is* my experiencing a red billiard ball. Why think that these must be alike? I am looking at a red billiard ball. You are looking at my experience of a red billiard ball, a brain process. What *would* be surprising is your experience's being anything at all like mine, your seeing a red spherical object in my brain.

Yes, but what about all those qualities of my experience? These seem altogether unlike any conceivable brain qualities. In experiencing the ball, I undergo a red experience, I savor phenomenal red. The ball's redness is a secondary quality, something in me, not in the ball. How could *that* be in my brain, the components of which possess only primary qualities?

Here again, distinguishing primary and secondary qualities by banishing secondary qualities to a nonmaterial mind is what is calling the shots. If you reject this, the argument does not take hold.

When you, or I, or anyone else, has a visual experience of a red billiard ball, it is the ball, not the experience, that is red. All parties agree that the ball, not the experience, is spherical, so why not treat the ball's color in the same way? U. T. Place (1924–2000) called the fallacy of mistaking qualities of an object experienced (qualities of the ball) for qualities of the experience of that object (your conscious visual experience of the ball), the "phenomenological fallacy." Your experience of a red billiard ball is neither spherical nor red. Talk of red *qualia* and of "phenomenal red" is simply one manifestation of the phenomenological fallacy.

What about Mary? Suppose Jackson is right: the most brilliant of scientists would be at a loss to work out what my experience of a red billiard ball is like by observing my brain. This would seem to disarm the phenomenological fallacy. Now the focus shifts from the ball's qualities to the qualities of experiences: *what it is like* to undergo those experiences, what it is like for someone to have a visual experience of a red billiard ball, for instance.

*Could* your observation of an occurrence in my brain be an observation of my experience? Certainly you could not work out *what it is like* for me to undergo the experience by observing my brain. But what does that show? Consider how you learn what something is like, what it is like to do a back flip, for instance. You could observe someone doing back flips, make videos, study the physiology of back flipping, but this would not tell you what it is like to do a back flip. To learn what it is like, you would need to do, or at least attempt, a back flip.

Knowing what it is like to do anything whatsoever requires doing it or doing something very like it. By doing it, you do not gain admission to an invisible realm. Knowing what it is like to see a red billiard ball is not to acquire a piece of factual knowledge inaccessible otherwise; it is just to experience – or to have experienced – a red billiard ball.

## 9.8  Sensitivity Training

The Hard Problem casts a shadow over contemporary discussions of conscious experiences and their qualitative character. Maybe I have said enough to convince you that the pull of Hard Problem has its origins in a lack of curiosity about a bevy of metaphysical presuppositions. In that regard, the Hard Problem, in common with many characteristically philosophical problems, is of our own making. In philosophy, as in chess, the first moves serve to constrain subsequent moves.

If you start with the assumption that qualities are found only in the mind, or that qualities of conscious experiences, *qualia*, are nonmaterial, "phenomenal" apparitions, you will have set the stage for the Hard

Problem. If you then accept that our inability to learn what it is like to undergo a particular experience by observing occurrences in brains shows that experiential qualities are nonmaterial, you will have arrived at your destination, the Hard Problem, the end of the line.

Although the Hard Problem is distinctively philosophical, it is not confined to philosophy and philosophers. A recurring theme in this book is that metaphysics is everywhere. Some of the most vocal parties in discussions of the Hard Problem are scientists. Almost everyone sees the Hard Problem as a problem, maybe even the hardest problem.

The point of my calling into question assumptions on which the Hard Problem rests has been to help you appreciate the reach of metaphysics. Your thoughts, no less than mine or anyone else's, are metaphysically tinged. Problems arise when metaphysical theses are unacknowledged or repressed.

The solution? Know thyself!

## Glossary

*Downward causation.* The idea, often mooted in discussions of emergence, that some wholes can exert "downward" "configurational" forces on their parts that outstrip forces the parts exert on one another.

*Dualism.* Proponents of dualism hold that minds and their contents are nonmaterial. The universe includes, in addition to material bodies, nonmaterial mental entities.

*Emergence.* A *strongly emergent* property would be a property of an emergent whole, a whole that is something in addition to its parts arranged as they are. In contrast, something is *weakly emergent* in a complex system if truths about it cannot be deduced from truths about its parts and their relations. Unlike strong emergence, weak emergence carries no metaphysical implications concerning emergent wholes.

*Epiphenomenalism.* Mental phenomena – colorful visual experiences, for instance – are by-products of neurological mechanisms that play no role in the operation of the mechanisms from which they issue. The ticking noise produced by a mechanical clock is a by-product of the clock's operation, one that contributes nothing to its operation.

*The Hard Problem.* The problem of understanding how conscious phenomena are related to material goings-on.

*Homunculus.* A tiny imaginary agent residing in your brain whose job it is to observe, perhaps on a miniature biological television screen, your experienced qualities, and direct your brain to issue appropriate motor commands to your body. The idea is that, if an account of conscious experiences relies on the postulation of a homunculus, this is enough to show that the theory is a nonstarter.

*Materialism.* In contrast to dualism, materialism holds that all there is are material objects and properties. Talk of minds should be understood as an indirect way of talking about material systems such as brains.

*Panpsychism.* The view that conscious qualities are not epiphenomenal or emergent, but pervade matter: conscious agents are made up of the same materials that make up everything else. Matter has a distinctive qualitative nature, perhaps "flickers" of consciousness, so that, when it is appropriately organized, the result is a fully conscious being.

*Phenomenal properties.* Properties of conscious experiences, also called *qualia*.

*Phenomenological fallacy.* The mistake of attributing qualities of experienced objects to experiences of those objects. When you experience a red ball, it is the ball, not your experience, that is red and spherical.

*Primary* and *secondary qualities.* Primary qualities are those identified by the physical sciences in investigating the universe. These include shape, size, mass, charge. Secondary qualities are taken to reside, not in material

objects, but in the minds of observers: perceived colors, heard sounds, smelt smells, feelings of warmth.
*Qualia.* Plural of *quale.* Characteristics of conscious experiences, perceived redness, for instance phenomenal redness.

## Further Readings

Two historical reflections on the problem are definitely worth a look: Wallace Matson's "Why Isn't the Mind–Body Problem Ancient?" that appeared in a collection edited by Paul Feyerabend and Grover Maxwell, *Mind, Matter, and Method: Essays in Philosophy and Science in Honor of Herbert Feigl* (Minneapolis, MN: University of Minnesota Press, 1966: 92–102); and Peter King's "Why Isn't the Mind–Body Problem Medieval?" in a collection edited by Henrik Lagerlund, *Forming the Mind: Essays on the Internal Senses and the Mind/Body Problem from Avicenna to the Medical Enlightenment* (Berlin: Springer, 2007: 187–205).

The Hard Problem was so-named by David Chalmers; see his *The Conscious Mind: In Search of a Fundamental Theory* (New York: Oxford University Press, 1996). Panpsychism has lately become something of an industry. Chalmers discusses panpsychism in *The Conscious Mind*, and, more recently, in "Panpsychism and Panprotopsychism," which is included in Torin Alter and Yujin Nagasawa, eds., *Consciousness in the Physical World: Perspectives on Russellian Monism* (New York: Oxford University Press, 2015: 246–76). Readers interested in the topic would be well served by Galen Strawson's *Real Materialism and Other Essays* (Oxford: Clarendon Press, 2008).

Strawson regards emergence as a non-starter, unlike Roger Sperry, who is quoted in the chapter; see his "A Modified Concept of Consciousness" (*Psychological Review* 76 [1969]: 532–6). Jaegwon Kim, in "Emergence:

Core Ideas and Issues" (*Synthese*, 151 [2006]: 347–54), is useful and accessible, as is Chalmers' "Strong and Weak Emergence," which appears in a collection edited by Philip Clayton and Paul Davies, *The Re-Emergence of Emergence* (Oxford: Oxford University Press, 2006: 244–55). Another useful collection: Mark Bedau and Paul Humphreys, *Emergence: Contemporary Readings in Philosophy and Science* (Cambridge, MA: MIT Press, 2008).

Mary, the brilliant scientist takes center stage in Frank Jackson's influential "Epiphenomenal Qualia" (*Philosophical Quarterly* 32 [1982]: 127–36), which has been widely reprinted. Colin McGinn "Can We Solve the Mind–Body Problem?" (*Mind* 98 [1989]: 349–66) poses the question, "how can Technicolor phenomenology arise from soggy grey matter?" See also David Chalmers's *The Character of Consciousness* (Oxford: Oxford University Press, 2010).

The focus on "what it is like" stems from Thomas Nagel's use of the phrase in a 1974 article, "What Is It Like to Be a Bat?" (*Philosophical Review* 83 [1974]: 435–50). Although Nagel is commonly regarded as the source of philosophical attention on the what-it's-like-ness of conscious experiences, B. A. Farrell had deployed the phrase in a paper published in 1950, "Experience" (*Mind* 59 [1950]: 170–98). Ullin Place, in "Is Consciousness a Brain Process?" (*British Journal of Psychology* 47 [1956]: 44–50) introduced the "phenomenological fallacy," and it plays a central role in J. J. C. Smart's "Sensations and Brain Processes" (*Philosophical Review* 68 [1959]: 141–56). Both of these papers proved influential in the subsequent debate over the nature of consciousness.

# 10

# Free Will

## 10.0 Acting Freely

Sometimes we act freely and are justly held account-
able for what we have done or set out to do. We hold
one another responsible for many of our actions. We
sometimes act unwillingly – when we are threatened, for
instance. Sometimes there are mitigating circumstances
– while walking down the footpath you are distracted
by a loud noise and collide with an elderly grandmother,
sending her sprawling. Sometimes you are not yourself
– you sleepwalk or succumb to a fever that makes you
delirious. In such cases, we typically withhold or moder-
ate our assessments of responsibility.

Social psychologists have established that we are subject to all manner of biases and, as a result, much less in
control of our thoughts and judgments than we might
have imagined. Psychoanalysis suggests that many of
our decisions are affected by repressed wishes and fears.

All of these factors – and you can undoubtedly think
of many more – mean that we are more constrained in
our choices than we would like to think, but even taken

together they do not altogether abolish *free will*. We freely choose courses of action at least some of the time, or so we believe.

What makes a choice a free choice, an exercise of free will? Philosophers have written extensively on the topic, setting out conditions for what constitutes a free action. Many of these conditions resemble those to which we commonly appeal in deciding whether someone is fully or partly responsible for some action, whether praise or blame is appropriate. Jurisprudential accounts supplement commonsense standards by introducing new subtleties. Sometimes the law prescribes explicit standards that are meant to regiment something close to what we generally mean when we judge someone to be responsible for some action.

One ingredient in the ordinary conception of free will is that a free action is uncoerced. We accept that, if you act under pressure at gunpoint, or if someone kidnaps a close friend and threatens the friend's life unless you do something you would never have done otherwise, your action is not free. Nor would an action be free were it performed as a result of brainwashing.

These are concrete examples, but what is the underlying principle? An action is free only if you did it because you chose to do it: you willed it. You did not choose to knock the grandmother over. A loud noise intervened, and your act was accidental, not deliberate, not done because you chose to do it. When you act under threat, however, you choose to act as you do because you have compelling reasons to do so, yet it is unlikely that anyone would blame you for your action. Although acting as you choose might be part of the story, it cannot be the whole story.

Perhaps what is missing is something to the effect that when you acted as you did, alternatives were open to you, alternatives you could easily have chosen. Often this is expressed counterfactually: an action is free, if you could have done otherwise had you so chosen.

This seems right for some cases, but what of actions performed under threat? You could have acted differently, alternatives were open to you, but under the circumstances, you would have been hard-pressed to have chosen to act in any other way. A threat does not eradicate, but effectively limits, your options. In such a case, you could not bring yourself to act on any of these alternatives other than the one on which you acted.

## 10.1 Is Free Will an Illusion?

Much more could be said about the conception – or conceptions – of free will most of us would accept. Most of us would accept that as we move through life, we routinely take and assess responsibility for actions we regard as freely performed. We do this despite lacking a complete account of what choosing and acting freely boils down to. We lack an explicit "real definition" of freedom (§6.0).

Once you leave everyday judgments behind and turn to the metaphysics of free will, however, the conversation shifts dramatically. In everyday life, we are guided by intuitions concerning what it takes to choose and act freely. Metaphysics offers hope that we can move beyond intuition to firmer ground. Intuitions can be in conflict and, in some cases, fail to issue decisive verdicts. If, as seems likely, the concept of free will is vague, there are going to be borderline cases that yield conflicting judgments.

Vagueness can be tolerated provided there are enough clear cases to serve as benchmarks. The question is, *are* there any clear cases; indeed, are there any cases of free will *at all*?

Who could doubt that there are? Whenever you need a reason to doubt something apparently plausible, look to philosophy.

Suppose the universe were of the kind depicted by

Spinoza (§8.5)? In Spinoza's universe everything that happens does so of necessity. Spinoza's universe is rigidly deterministic, apparently leaving no room for free will. Our sense that we, on occasion, choose and act freely is an illusion, an adaptive illusion perhaps, but nevertheless an illusion.

You might think that Spinoza poses no real threat. In the first place, we have every reason to accept that we sometimes choose freely, that we are sometimes responsible for what we do. This, coupled with the fact that there are options to Spinoza – Hume, for instance – means that we can, in good conscience, set Spinoza aside. A Humean discards the thought that anything necessitates anything, everything is "loose and separate." This leaves ample room for free will.

Looked at more closely, however, the Spinoza–Hume divide proves difficult to make out (see §§8.4–8.5). Hume abolishes necessary connections among the occupants of the universe, but Spinoza does the same. For Spinoza, the universe, the One, evolves as it does of its own accord. But individual entities – modes – do not bring about changes in other individual entities. This sounds like Hume, but why think that Hume is party to Spinoza's necessitarianism?

David Lewis spells it out. You have qualities distributed in spacetime, perhaps qualities *of* spacetime. The thought that you could have been different than you are, or that you could have failed to exist, is transformed into the thought that a situation in which someone very like you is different, or one in which you are absent, is *similar* to the actual situation. Strictly speaking, nothing could have been other than it is. This sounds like Spinoza.

Free will is in trouble.

What about the Aristotelian option? A pluralistic Aristotelian universe includes configurations of empowered objects interacting in ways that affect one another and result in new configurations. The universe is this evolving configuration, later states being brought about by earlier states. In allowing for genuine interactions among objects, an Aristotelian differs from both Spinoza and Hume. Does Aristotelianism open the door to free will?

On the Aristotelian model, objects' interactions are manifestations of their powers. The identity of a power, its nature, is fixed by what it is a power *for* (with various reciprocal powers). If a billiard ball's sphericality empowers it to roll when set in motion on smooth surfaces (providing they are not *too* smooth), then if you set the ball in motion, you have its rolling. The ball's failing to roll would indicate either that sphericality does not, after all, equip spherical things to roll or, more likely, some additional power is on hand that, in concert with the ball's nature, results in the ball's remaining stationary. Were the ball made of steel, the addition of a powerful magnet to the setup could ensure such an outcome.

In an Aristotelian universe, then, necessitation remains, relocated in individual objects. Given your current state and the conditions in which you find yourself, anything you do is a manifestation of the evolving causal matrix in which you are embedded. Your choosing to do one thing rather than another is entirely a consequence of your location in this matrix.

It might be an open question whether Aristotle, Hume, or Spinoza is right about the universe in which we reside, but it appears not to be an open question whether, given the initial state of the universe, anything could have been in any way different than it is. (A reminder: I am using Aristotle, Hume, and Spinoza, not to refer to the philosophers themselves, but as labels for ways of thinking about the universe loosely associated with the historical Aristotle, Hume, and Spinoza.)

## 10.2 Spontaneity

Maybe there is still hope for free will, however. The universes of Aristotle, Hume, and Spinoza might not be the only options. Physics tells us that some elements are unstable (§5.5). They decay unpredictably over some extended period of time. When an element decays, its decaying is not brought about by anything, its decaying is *spontaneous*.

What happens if you add unstable elements to an Aristotelian universe? You have a deterministic causal matrix. Here and there are spontaneous occurrences. These can have effects in the matrix, so, taken as a whole, it is no longer deterministic. (I leave it to you the reader to work out whether, and if so, how, the universes of Spinoza and Hume might accommodate unstable elements.)

Might this provide an opening for free will? On a conventional Aristotelian picture, whatever you do is a straightforward consequence of your place in an unrelenting causal matrix. Suppose you sprinkle in spontaneous occurrences. These affect the way the matrix evolves. You are still bound by your place in the matrix, however. How would adding minute spontaneous occurrences involving unstable elements be supportive of free will?

Suppose, however, your *will* could act spontaneously, on the model of an unstable element? When your will acts spontaneously – in choosing to do one thing rather than another, for instance – its choosing is uncaused. This would not make your choice "random." Just as the decay of a radium atom is constrained by the nature of the atom, the character of your choice might be shaped by your psychological makeup (§8.1).

This would liberate your will from the causal matrix, but it would threaten free choices in another way. When you choose freely, you need not be acting impulsively, your choice need not resemble the spontaneous decay of a radium atom. You are acting, in part, because you have reasons to do so, and to do so *now*. When you act *for* a reason, when you act *because* you have reasons to so act, your reasons would seem to play a role in the production of the act. Were your choice unaffected by your reasons, it might be spontaneous, but it would no longer be reasoned. In an important respect, a choice spontaneous in this way would not be *your* choice. You would find yourself suddenly choosing one thing rather than another, but you would be alienated from the choice.

The situation appears hopeless. No matter how you slice it, we seem little more than puppets manipulated by forces beyond our control. Peter van Inwagen sums it up nicely:

> If determinism is true, then our acts are the consequences of the laws of nature and events in the remote past. But it is not up to us what went on before we were born, and neither is it up to us what the laws of nature are. Therefore the consequences of these things (including our present acts) are not up to us. (*An Essay on Free Will*: 16)

Although van Inwagen mentions determinism, allowing spontaneous, uncaused occurrences into the picture does little to blunt its force.

## 10.3 Approaches to Free Will

You are now well into the rabbit hole of the metaphysics of free will. We began with innocent ideas about free choice, but those innocent ideas, when pushed, fell to pieces. Philosophers who have thought long and hard about the nature of free will have yet to achieve consensus. I shall mention three influential approaches to the topic.

First, some philosophers, the *hard incompatibilists*,

deny that we have free will. As the consequence argument makes abundantly clear, free will is, as a matter of fact, incompatible with determinism even when this is tempered by the kind of spontaneity encountered in physics. Free will is a kind of illusion, a story we tell ourselves that provides some level of comfort, but one that ultimately lacks credibility.

Second, *libertarians* insist that free will is a given. Skeptics about free will – incompatibilists, for instance – cannot really doubt that they, at least sometimes, choose freely. Skeptics might profess to doubt free will, but their own behavior belies this doubt. Everyone, skeptics included, deliberates over courses of action before deciding how to act. Deliberation would be pointless, however, unless you accepted free will. The moral of van Inwagen's consequence argument is not that we lack free will, but that agents acting freely manage somehow to elude the causal matrix. Incompatibilists focus on the apparent fact that we are merely cogs in a complex causal machine. In contrast, libertarians argue that we have much better reason to believe in free will than in any cosmology that renders free will impossible.

This might seem to exhaust the possibilities, but there is an influential third position, *compatibilism*. Compatibilists agree with the incompatibilists that the causal matrix is inescapable, but deny that this shows that we lack free will. They agree, as well, with the libertarians, that we do sometimes choose freely, but deny that this would require our escaping the causal matrix. Free will is *compatible* with determinism.

How might that work? Suppose you revert to a hierarchical conception of reality as depicted in §3.4. The sciences, and especially physics, describe a fundamental level of reality, but there are many less-than-fundamental levels. Biology and psychology describe successively higher levels. Higher levels are dependent on, yet distinct from, successively lower levels. Free will would seem to have a place on the psychological level. Just as

Eddington's everyday Table No. 1 depends on, without being reducible to, his scientific Table No. 2, so psychological states, including those implicated in free choices, depend on, without being reducible to, states of brains, and ultimately interactive collections of particles.

This, at any rate, is one way to frame compatibilism. Physics presides over a largely deterministic realm, a causal matrix in which you are embedded, but there are, in addition, psychological and social realms that admit free choice.

Libertarians are right to point out that, outside the seminar room, no one is an incompatibilist. Just as on the battlefield there are no atheists, there are no practicing incompatibilists. Incompatibilists counter that libertarians appear to be engaged in special pleading. We have an apparent standoff. If a scientifically respectable cosmology and free will are incompatible, something has to give. For hard incompatibilists what gives is free will; for libertarians cosmology is what gives. Faced with a dilemma in which so much is at stake, where do *you* stand?

Compatibilists endeavor to go between the horns of the dilemma. The mistake, they contend, is to surrender to the consequence argument and imagine that determinism and free will are irreconcilable. Once you put this assumption aside, you can eat your cake and have it. In response, opponents of compatibilism argue that compatibilists "solve" the problem of free will by failing to take it seriously.

It will not have escaped the astute reader that all sides here take for granted that you are in a position to weigh up the evidence and, on the basis of that evidence, determine where you stand. Such an assumption would be hard to credit if you doubted free will. This suggests a prior commitment to free will of a kind that renders the debate pointless.

You are probably thinking, "Well of course! It's all just metaphysical rubbish!" If you are honest, however, you will admit that, once you become aware of the tension between physics and free will, the toothpaste is out of the tube. You have taken a bite of the apple and lost your innocence.

## 10.4  Reconciliation

The situation appears dire. You could always simply put aside thoughts about the status of free will and go about business as usual. I daresay most of us do, most of the time. It would be salutary, however, if we could retain our complacency in good conscience.

Think back to the discussion of the reconciliation project in chapter 3. This is the project of coming to terms somehow with the apparent clash between Wilfrid Sellars's manifest and scientific images. In the case of free will, we have, on the one hand, our everyday picture of the universe and our place in it and, on the other hand, scientifically informed cosmology. These appear irreconcilable.

Bear in mind that the manifest image shapes not only everyday life, but also the practices of scientists working with sophisticated instruments in their laboratories. The manifest image is not to be trifled with – but neither is the scientific image.

In the course of a discussion of Eddington's two tables in chapter 3, I surveyed three approaches to the reconciliation project.

(1)  The manifest image is a fiction; reality is what emanates from the scientific image. (Eddington's Table No. 1, the everyday table, is an illusion; only the scientific table, Table No. 2, is real.)

(2)  Reality resides with the manifest image; the scientific image is useful instrumentally, but not literally true. (Table No. 2, the scientific table, is a "construct," something invented to enable us to find our way

around in a universe comprising familiar everyday objects including Table No. 1.)
(3) The manifest image encompasses higher-level, less-than-fundamental realities rooted in a fundamental reality addressed by the scientific image. (The scientific table is a fundamental constituent of the universe; Table No. 1 is a higher-level entity, dependent on, but distinct from, Table No. 2.)

My suggestion in §3.6 was that there is a fourth option:

(4) The scientific image affords an account of the nature of the truthmakers for truths at home in the manifest image. (Eddington's Table no. 2 purports to be an account of the nature of the truthmaker for truths about his everyday Table No. 1.)

You can see counterparts of (1)–(3) reflected in the three attempts to solve the problem of free will introduced earlier.

(1*) Free will is a fiction; reality is what issues from the scientific image and that is incompatible with free will (hard incompatibilism).
(2*) Free will is nonnegotiable; when it comes to human action the scientific image is useful instrumentally, but not literally true (libertarianism).
(3*) Free will is at home in the company of higher-level, less-than-fundamental realities rooted in a fundamental reality addressed by the scientific image (compatibilism).

Applying (4) to the problem of free will:

(4*) The scientific image affords an account of the nature of the truthmakers for truths concerning free will belonging to the manifest image.

Does (4) amount to nothing more than a disingenuous version of compatibilism? Maybe not.

In making a case for (4), I suggested that (1)–(3) erred in comparing truths expressed in a vocabulary tailored to the manifest image directly with truths expressed in a vocabulary suited for physics. The mismatch led philosophers to argue that one or the other collection of truths must be abandoned – options (1) and (2) – or taken to be true of distinct realities – option (3). Following my suggestion, suppose that there is but one reality, variously describable. Talk of the manifest and scientific images is simply a very general way of acknowledging this thought. The manifest and scientific images are neither in competition, nor do they encompass distinct realities.

Motion and the passage of time provide an illustration. Suppose that, when it is true that a billiard ball rolls across a billiard table, physics tells us that what happens is analogous to what happens when a cursor moves across your laptop's screen. You do not have an object occupying successive regions of space over time. You have a succession of stationary thickenings in space analogous to a succession of stationary pixels turning on and off.

My contention was that it would be a mistake to think that this would be at odds with our observation of the moving ball. It is true that the ball moves, but physics provides an account of what billiard ball motion *is*, the nature of the truthmakers for claims about moving billiard balls. These truthmakers might include nothing that moves.

If something like this were right, it would extend naturally to free will. It is true that we choose and act freely from time to time. You can point to instances, cases in which an agent apparently freely chooses to act in a particular way and so acts. It could, however, turn out that the nature of truthmakers for truths about free will are wholly deterministic.

This is not compatibilism. Compatibilism about motion would require that the ball's moving is compatible with its remaining stationary on the billiard table. No, the billiard ball moves, but the nature of truthmakers for this truth – what it is for the ball to move – might turn out to include nothing that moves.

Similarly, compatibilism about free will would be the view that your choice's being free is compatible with its being determined by factors over which you have no control, and that is not what (4*) says. No, your *choice* is free, but the nature of the truthmakers for this truth – what it *is* for you to have chosen as you did on this occasion – could turn out to include no spontaneous, undetermined, unnecessitated elements.

You might or might not agree with this approach to free will. The discussion will have served its purpose, however, if it has given you something to think about and thereby reinforced the book's guiding theme: *like it or not, metaphysics is not going away.*

## Glossary

*Compatibilism*. Free will is compatible with – and maybe even presupposes – determinism. The idea that we must choose between free will and determinism is founded on a misunderstanding of what is required for free will.

*Hard incompatibilism*. The universe as depicted by physics is deterministic, but free will is incompatible with determinism, so free will is an illusion.

*Libertarianism*. In the context of discussions of free will, the view that, although free will is incompatible with determinism, we have excellent reasons to regard some of our choices as free, so determinism must be false, at least when it comes to agents choosing freely.

## Further Readings

The consequence argument was introduced to contemporary readers by Peter van Inwagen in *An Essay on Free Will* (Oxford: Clarendon Press, 1983). In "Some Thoughts on *An Essay on Free Will*" (*Harvard Review of Philosophy* 22 [2015]: 16–30), van Inwagen himself provides an excellent summary of his position.

Galen Strawson, in "The Bounds of Freedom" in Robert Kane, ed., *The Oxford Handbook of Free Will* (Oxford: Oxford University Press, 2002: 441–60), argues that free will is impossible *whether or not* determinism is true. To be free is to be responsible for your actions, but that would require your being responsible for your being in the state of mind that issued in your action. This leads to a regress – to be responsible for that state of mind, you would have to be responsible for whatever state of mind led to it, and so on.

In *Free Will, Agency, and Meaning in Life* (Oxford: Oxford University Press, 2014), Derk Pereboom argues that free will would require a kind of spontaneity we almost certainly lack. Pereboom calls his position "hard incompatibilism." For a very different view, see John Martin Fischer, *My Way: Essays on Moral Responsibility* (New York: Oxford University Press, 2006).

Please do not make the mistake of confusing libertarians about free will with social and political libertarians. The two species of libertarianism are unrelated, at least to the extent that you could be a libertarian about free will without being a political libertarian. (I am unsure whether the opposite holds.)

Robert Kane's *The Significance of Free Will* (New York: Oxford University Press, 1996) offers one kind of libertarian account of free will. E. J. Lowe, in *Personal Agency: The Metaphysics of Mind and Action* (Oxford: Oxford University Press, 2008), and Timothy O'Connor, in *Persons and Causes: The Metaphysics of Free Will* (New York: Oxford University Press, 2000), defend distinctive accounts centered on agents. In *Libertarian Accounts of Free Will* (Oxford: Oxford University Press, 2003), Randolph Clarke takes up a range of competing libertarian approaches. Alfred Mele, in *Free Will and Luck* (Oxford: Oxford University Press, 2006), in addition to offering an important response to Strawson, lucidly scrutinizes both compatibilism and libertarianism.

Although "compatibilism" has a long history, the proximate source is probably Dickinson S. Miller (writing under the pseudonym, R. E. Hobart), "Free Will as Involving Determination and Inconceivable Without It" (*Mind*, 43 [1934]: 1–27); see also Daniel Dennett, *Elbow Room: The Varieties of Free Will Worth Wanting* (Cambridge, MA: MIT Press, 1984). John Martin Fischer and Mark Ravizza's *Responsibility and Control: A Theory of Moral Responsibility* (Cambridge: Cambridge University Press, 1998) promotes an influential compatibilist line.

# 11

# Are We There Yet?

## 11.0 No Pain No Gain

If you have made it this far, you are to be commended.
I have tried your patience and tested your endurance.
Think of what you have been through as a metaphysics
boot camp designed to sharpen your appreciation of the
subject, and toughen your philosophical sinews.

Rest assured that I am not going to stir anything further into the mix. You already have more than enough
to chew on. As I have insisted throughout the book, the
aim has not been simply to march you through a catalogue of metaphysical topics. The topics introduced and
my way of discussing them were meant to be illustrative. If you are a student using this book as a textbook,
you will already be aware that your instructor does not
always agree with the lines I take on particular topics.
That is philosophy for you.

You would, however, be wrong to conclude from the
fact that philosophers can disagree on almost anything,
that there is no there there, or to conclude that truth
in philosophy is relative: what is true for me need not

be true for you. Philosophical disagreement can mask wide avenues of agreement. My discussion of a surprising convergence of Hume and Spinoza was taken up to illustrate precisely this point. Once you look below the surface, you can see that this is the rule, not the exception.

## 11.1 Truthmaking Again

The notion of truthmaking was introduced in §3.7: when a judgment, or belief, or theory purporting to trivialize the universe is true, something, some way the universe is, makes it true. The truthmaker for "the sky is blue" is the sky's being blue. The truthmaker for "the billiard ball is rolling" is the billiard ball's rolling. In a Newtonian universe the truthmaker for "objects attract with a force proportional to the product of their respective masses and inversely proportional to the square of their distance apart" would be, not simply objects behaving in accordance with the law, but the empowering nature of mass. Owing to their masses, objects would exert forces on one another that would, in the absence of competing forces, lead them to "obey" the law.

It goes without saying that you can know what the truthmaker is for some truth without knowing much about the nature of that truthmaker. "The sky is blue" is made true by the sky's being blue, but what this is would be complicated to spell out. You can know that "The billiard ball is rolling" is made true by the billiard ball's rolling, but what *that* amounts to remains an open question.

Truthmaking underlies what I have called ontologically serious metaphysics. If you back an assertion that bears on the universe, you should be prepared to say what the truthmakers for that assertion are or might be.

You can see how this works in the case of causation.

Some philosophers explicate causation by appealing to contrary-to-the-fact conditionals, counterfactuals. If C causes E, then, had C not occurred, E would not have occurred. This, suitably qualified to accommodate more complex cases, seems right. But if it is right, it is fair to ask, when a counterfactual is true, what makes it true? You could, for instance, point to powers possessed by interacting objects. The sugar would have dissolved in your cup of tea had you spooned it into your cup. What makes this true might be powers inherent in the sugar and the tea.

In saying this, you might or might not be right, but you are at least being ontologically serious – as you would not be had you left the counterfactuals "dangling," untethered to the universe: they are true, but not made true by any way the universe is. Nor would it be ontologically serious to trivialize the truthmaker: what makes the counterfactual true is a contrary-to-the-fact fact.

## 11.2 Realism

By taking seriously the need for truthmakers, you help ensure that metaphysics engages with reality. This should not come as a revelation. The notion that metaphysical claims call for truthmakers is simply an extension of more widespread practices in the sciences and elsewhere. You test a scientific claim by finding out whether the universe is as it is claimed to be. It might take a lot more to discover what the universe's being this way amounts to. That is a job for the sciences, and, in particular, physics, but physics is a work-in-progress.

The significance of truthmaking stems from a commitment to realism about a particular subject matter. Claims about the universe are claims as to how things are, independently of how we happen to think about or describe them. You are a realist about electrons, for instance, if you think that there are indeed electrons "out there" and these are what makes assertions about electrons true (or false). Electron anti-realism would reconstrue claims about electrons as *façons de parler*, figurative expressions, useful for the purposes of calculation and prediction, but not meant to be taken literally.

The second response to the question of the relation of Eddington's two tables exemplifies one form of scientific anti-realism.

(2) Reality resides with the manifest image; the scientific image is useful instrumentally, but not literally true. (Table No. 2, the scientific table, is a "construct," something invented to enable us to find our way around in a universe comprising familiar everyday objects including Table No. 1.)

On the face of it, this would seem to amount to realism about tables and anti-realism about electrons. On another reading, however, the response has it that all there is to tables are our perceptions of them. This reading, associated with Berkeley and discussed in §3.1, is anti-realist about tables. Assertions about tables are not made true by mind-independent objects, tables, but by perceptions, and these belong to the mind.

This kind of anti-realism does not simply deny the existence of mind-independent tables, however. The thought, rather, is that the very idea of mind-independent objects "outside," but corresponding to, our perceptions is incoherent. While he is an anti-realist about material objects, Berkeley is a realist about minds and their contents. Anti-realism about some domain requires realism about some other.

Realism is not all or nothing. You can be a realist about tables, but not about numbers, for instance. To be a realist about numbers would be to accept that truths involving numbers, mathematical truths, have truthmakers, numbers. Similarly, if you are a realist about the past or the future, you assume that there are truthmakers for assertions about the past or the future. Moral realists think that there are distinctively moral truthmakers for moral judgments.

## 11.3 Ontological Seriousness

These are difficult matters, but you are not being asked to decide whether you are a realist or an anti-realist about morals, or numbers, or the past and future. I am simply pointing out that, when you think that a judgment on a metaphysical matter purports to be about things as they are independently of how we think they are, you are taking up a realist attitude toward the target of that judgment. When you do this, you are committed to there being objective mind-independent truthmakers for the judgment. The point applies to thoughts themselves. Your thoughts are what they are independently of how you think they are.

Truthmaking might seem supremely uninteresting. Who could doubt that, when a judgment expresses a truth concerning a way the universe is, it has a truthmaker? You would do well, however, to keep this in mind should you elect to delve more deeply into metaphysical topics. Earlier I noted that some philosophers explain causation by appealing to counterfactuals: causation is given a counterfactual gloss or "analysis." If this is an advance, however, it behooves those embracing it to come clean and say what the truthmakers for counterfactuals are. Failure to do so, while common, manifests a lack of ontological seriousness.

Some readers might question my charge of ontological frivolity here. Many philosophers are happy to provide truthmakers for counterfactuals by invoking alternative universes ("possible worlds"). Channeling David Lewis, they accept that a counterfactual – had C not occurred, E would not have occurred – is true when, in universes most similar to ours in which a twin (a "counterpart") of $C$ fails to occur, a twin of $E$ fails to occur as well. So the truthmakers for counterfactual truths are all those alternative universes. Ontological seriousness is back!

Two comments are in order here. First, this is probably not how Lewis himself saw it. He is clear that truthmakers for truths that have truthmakers are to be found here in our universe, the "actual" universe.

> The character of our world ... makes the counterfactual true. But it is only by bringing the other worlds into the story that we can say in any concise way what character it takes to make the counterfactual true. The other worlds provide a frame of reference whereby we can characterise our world. (*Philosophical Papers*, vol. 2: 22)

Alternative universes provide a "frame of reference" for modal assertions. In evaluating a counterfactual – had $C$ not occurred, $E$ would not have occurred – you are looking for situations similar to the actual situation in what you judge to be relevant respects.

The first point to notice, then, is that Lewis himself does not think the alternative universes function as truthmakers for truths pertaining to our universe. The second point is that, in most cases, this is irrelevant. Many philosophers who invoke alternative universes profess to be anti-realists about them. Alternative universes are useful fictions, the usefulness of which does not require that they exist.

This, however, would undercut any pretext of ontological seriousness. Without truthmakers, how could counterfactuals tell us anything about how things are? The point extends to modal truths, generally, truths about contingency, possibility, necessity, and their contraries. If you explicate these by invoking alternative universes, "possible worlds," then declare that these are only useful fictions, you ought to be ashamed – or at least embarrassed!

## 11.4 What Now?

I am reasonably confident that anyone who has taken to heart the discussion in this and the preceding chapters would be equipped to think seriously about topics in metaphysics that I have not covered. Being equipped, even being well equipped is one thing; however, negotiating the terrain is something else altogether. No book could prepare you for the labyrinthine twists and turns characteristic of today's academic writing. In this regard philosophy is no worse than some disciplines and certainly better than others.

Should you decide – freely! – to dip into contemporary work in metaphysics, you will find it challenging. I have found myself unable to sleep at night wondering what advice I might have for readers interested in pursuing topics covered in this book and other topics in metaphysics. Much contemporary writing on metaphysical subjects is addressed to specialized academic audiences. Many discussions presuppose familiarity with a significant body of literature, and many are technical in nature. Each chapter of this book concludes with a list of suggested readings, chosen for their relative accessibility and linked to topics addressed in the chapter.

I was moved to write this book in part because I believe that the best way to ensure that you understand a difficult subject is to explain that subject to someone unfamiliar with it. Too often we think we understand something when really all we have are words, statements of positions, the familiarity of which means that we no longer need to think about them.

Even if you did not benefit from my efforts, then, I have. Scant consolation for you the reader, but we must learn to be grateful for small blessings.

You are hereby on your own.

Go well!

## Further Readings

The list of suggested readings for chapter 1 includes my best suggestions for anyone interested in pushing ahead solo. Readings associated with other chapters are more sharply focused on particular topics.

Contemporary metaphysics has been much invigorated by Australian philosophers. David Lewis, an American, had a special fondness for philosophy in Australia – and Australian footy (Lewis barracked for Essendon). D. C. Williams, another American, was influential in Australia and later influential outside Australia, chiefly owing to Keith Campbell – a Kiwi once based at Sydney University where he was a colleague of David Armstrong. J. J. C. Smart (1920–2012), born in Glasgow and educated at Oxford, spent his career in Australia, first at Adelaide – where his colleagues included C. B. Martin (an American expatriate), and Ullin Place (a British-born psychologist) – all three of whom featured importantly in this book.

If you are curious about Australian philosophy, a good place to start is Peter Godfrey Smith's "Australian Philosophy" (*Aeon*, 19 March 2019, https://aeon.co/essays/why-does-australia-have-an-outsized-influence-on-philosophy). For a more detailed history centered on the Sydney department, see James Franklin, *Corrupting the Youth: A History of Philosophy in Australia* (Sydney: Macleay Press, 2003). Graham Oppy and Nick Trakakis's *A Companion to Philosophy in Australia & New Zealand*, 2nd edn (Clayton, VIC: Monash University Publishing, 2014) is especially useful.

# Index

Entries that appear in the glossary are indicated by page numbers in bold.